PROPERTY AUCTIONS

PROPERTY AUCTIONS

Edited by

Clive Carpenter FRICS and Susan Harris

1988

THE ESTATES GAZETTE LIMITED
151 WARDOUR STREET, LONDON W1V 4BN

First published 1988
ISBN 0 7282 0114 3

© Leaf Coppin 1988

*This book was commissioned
and produced for the Estates Gazette Limited
by Leaf Coppin Limited*

Phototypeset by Input Typesetting Ltd., London
Printed at the Bath Press, Avon

Contents

		page
Introduction *Susan Harris*		vii
1. The Auction Department and the Auctioneer *Tony Trump* FRICS		1
2. Auction Preparation and Presentation *John Barnett* FRICS		15
3. Individual Residential Properties *Peter Kearon* FRICS		31
4. Residential Investment *Clifford G. Murphy* FRICS		41
5. Residential Land *Christopher Drury* FRICS		49
6. Commercial Property *Clive Carpenter* FRICS		59
7. Industrial Property *Christopher Drury* FRICS		69
8. Land, Agriculture and Sporting *J. P. H. Wiseman* FRICS		78
9. Conduct Unbecoming *Clive Carpenter* FRICS		92
10. The Future of the Property Auction *Janice McKenzie*		101
Appendix 1 The National Conditions of Sale (20th edition)		108
Appendix 2 General Conditions of Sale		120
Appendix 3 Typical Catalogue Entries and Special Conditions for Commercial Property		126
Appendix 4 Particulars and Special Conditions of Sale for a Country Residential Property		131
Appendix 5 Memoranda of Sale and Purchaser's Slip		140
Appendix 6 Catalogue Proof Check-List		143
Appendix 7 Extracts from Statutes		145
Index		156

Acknowledgements

The Editors would like to thank the following for their kind help in the preparation of the book: Derek Baldock FRICS, Michael Landers ARICS, Richard Pryce FRICS, John Trevor FRICS, Ray Richardson FRICS and the London Auction Mart.

Introduction

Susan Harris

The second oldest profession in the world is alleged to be that of auctioneer. An auction sale was recorded in the twenty-third chapter of the Book of Genesis, when Abraham bought the fields of Machpela from Ephron by giving his word in front of witnesses at the gates of the city. Unlike the oldest profession, however, auctioneering is perfectly legal and honourable, although some auctioneers would say less profitable! Women have featured as prominently in the history of auctioneering as in the 'other' profession: indeed, without them auctions might never have become an established method of sale. For it was women who initially formed the merchandise, to be purchased as slaves or wives, for the Roman auctions, which were a refinement, it seems, of Babylonian practice, dating back to at least 450 BC. The prime lots, the beauties, were offered at the beginning of the sale and were sold on an escalating scale, while the more 'difficult' lots were disposed of by a kind of reverse bidding. The same order of sale applies at property auctions today, with the prime lots at the beginning of the catalogue and the less significant ones at the end. The system has hardly changed, only the goods on offer.

Visitors to the building previously owned and occupied by the Chartered Auctioneers and Estate Agents' Institute, in Lincoln's Inn Fields, London, can see the auction immortalised in the form of two semi-circular murals above the

♦ INTRODUCTION ♦

glass doors on either side of the outer hall, depicting shapely ladies, exhibiting considerable charms, being sold into slavery by the candle method, whereby the successful bid was the last one before the wick spluttered into extinction.

Until the end of the eighteenth century, very few public auctions were concerned with land and buildings: goods and chattels were their stock-in-trade. By the mid-eighteenth century, enough auctions of various kinds had been held to warrant a legal definition of rights, duties and obligations for auctioneers, vendors and purchasers. In 1779, the Chancellor of the Exchequor considered there was sufficient activity in the field of auctioneering to justify introducing an Auctions and Sales tax. Far from discouraging the volume of sales by this method, the tax only served to increase the number of auctions which were held in packed coffee-houses. The most popular was Garroways in Cornhill, and particulars of a sale held there on 5 June 1803 (in the archives of Drivers Jonas), indicate that freehold and copyhold estates at Epping Nazeing and other Essex villages were offered.

The turn of the eighteenth century saw the first signs of auction legislation being brought in, and, in 1808, the first Auction Mart was created in a new building on the corner of Bartholomew Lane and Throgmorton Street in the City of London, with coffee rooms, offices, open galleries and many other facilities in addition to the sale room. Among early lots to be offered were a West Indian sugar plantation and Shakespeare's house at Stratford-upon-Avon. The Auction Mart survived until 1864 when the building was sold by tender, one of the four trustees achieving the sale being one Henry Christie of King Street, St. James's, Auctioneer.

While a second mart was found, sales were held in various places, notably at the London Tavern, the Masons' House Tavern and the Guildhall Tavern; and the habit of using taverns has never died out, with many smaller auctions continuing to be held in public houses all over the country.

In 1866, a new Auction Mart company was formed under the chairmanship of Frederick Chinnocks, other well-known

◆ INTRODUCTION ◆

directors including Frank Debenham and Robert River. A home was eventually found in Tokenhouse Yard and auctions started on the ground floor of the partially completed building in August 1867. The closing of Garroways coffee-house contributed to its success and the Mart flourished there until 1881, when 'a severe depression in all matters connected with land' occurred, and sales there, although satisfactory, suffered somewhat from this slump. Nonetheless, what are now household names in chartered surveying began to emerge as auctioneers in the late nineteenth century. Hillier Parker May & Rowden, for instance, commenced auctions at the Mart in 1896; and one of the earliest firms of auctioneers, H. E. Foster and Cranfield, established in 1843, specialists in reversions, life interests, insurance policies, endowment policies, and kindred matters, held sales there almost monthly. J. Trevor & Sons was also established in 1896, but did not begin auctions until 1919 from a sale room in Basil Street, when Colonel Jack Trevor started selling off surplus war goods on behalf of the government, and also held charity auctions.

In 1917, the Mart was severely damaged by enemy aircraft during a raid on the City, and in 1919, with affairs at a low ebb, the premises were sold to the Bank of England who bought out all the shareholders. Sales continued at Winchester House in Old Broad Street and in 1921 the London Auction Mart was formed, under the auspices of the Chartered Auctioneers and Estate Agents' Institute of the United Kingdom. They took premises at 155 Queen Victoria Street which was transformed into four auction rooms, the largest of which could seat a hundred and ten people; there was also a members' room, telephone boxes, a consulting room and various other offices.

Many members of both the profession and the public remember Queen Victoria Street with affection. One of its features was the number of auctions that took place every day, and some auctioneers recall bidders running from room to room. It was effectively the only venue at which to hold property auctions and, far from being restricted to London

♦ INTRODUCTION ♦

auctioneers, many practitioners from the provinces preferred to sell there in the belief that, although the property on offer was local, it would attract wider interest by being sold at the Mart – a view still held today.

The nineteen-twenties saw the foundation of present-day legislative controls with the Auctions (Bidding Agreements) Act 1927. This was fortified by the Mock Auctions Act 1961 and the Auctions (Bidding Agreements) Act 1969. The respectability of auctions was also enhanced when the Estate Exchange Ltd. entered into an agreement with the *Estates Gazette* in 1923 to record the weekly sales in the UK and even occasionally on the Continent. This arrangement has continued, with geographic variations, and nowadays information can be obtained on all sales which take place south of a line roughly from the Wash to Bristol.

In 1969 the Mart moved to Fur Trade House where the first sales were conducted on 16 October of that year: some five thousand properties at Hampstead Garden Suburb, in London, were offered and sold in one lot for £2.45 million, an outstanding amount and a record that was not broken for several years. The occasion was filmed by BBC Television and shown on both their evening news programmes.

Property sales had however fallen from favour in the course of the sixties, and gradually the word 'Auctioneer' which had once featured in most estate agents' windows disappeared. The Mart continued holding sales at Fur Trade House for 9 years, but there was a general decline in business. In an effort to reverse the fall in their fortune, it was decided to move into the West End of London and in 1978 the London Auction Mart chose the Connaught Rooms in Great Queen Street, off Kingsway, as its new home. Although many London firms have held their monthly and bi-monthly sales there, some prefer to hold their auctions in prestigious London hotels.

The London Auction Mart is run by a board of twenty-one nominated directors, all chartered surveyors and mainly auctioneers of leading London firms. Although the Mart is not restricted to members of the Royal Institute of Chartered

♦ INTRODUCTION ♦

Surveyors, in order to maintain a standard in the interests of the public and the profession, the board has the right to refuse an application to sell at the Mart if they think a prospective auction firm does not match the required standards.

The growth of the property auction market in the 1980s has been huge, as records of sales at the London Auction Mart and other venues confirm. The leading auction houses now between them dispose of almost every type of property throughout London and the UK, and sold over £500 million's worth under the hammer in 1987. The acceptable face of auctions has 'seen off' their reputation as solely a method of disposing of 'blighted' or difficult properties. Their position of importance and trust is reflected in the new 'mega-auction' where five or six hundred people attend a sale containing several hundred lots. A far cry from even ten years ago, when twenty or thirty buyers would turn up to bid for a dozen or so lots.

The acceptability of auctions is seen in the increasing number of institutional vendors who would previously have disposed of their property by private treaty or tender. Banks, local authorities, pension funds, nationalised industries such as British Rail and British Coal, and, more recently, building societies selling their foreclosures, have all become regular auction fans. The auction room is no longer the domain of the residential dealer anxious to unload his tacky stock on to some poor unsuspecting punter. Even the Metropolitan Police have sold their surplus blocks of flats this way.

These large vendors have paved the way for the owner-occupier and first-time buyer, who hitherto avoided auctions because of the dubious nature of the property. Now, the general property-buying public are to be seen buying and selling their own flats and houses under the hammer. Unmodernised flats and houses are the most popular residential lots, but tenants in occupation of properties being sold as investments are also beginning to come to the room and bid, their one and only chance of ever being able to buy their home of, usually, many years standing. Thus the residential

♦ INTRODUCTION ♦

dealer who once dominated this end of the market is being both outnumbered and outbid by such owner-occupiers and tenants in occupation, who are able to pay more since they do not have to make a profit on the resale as a dealer does. Such unmodernised property is limited (see chapter 4, below) and for many buyers it is the only way to secure it, private treaty agents often preferring to sell such stock to dealers who will reinstruct several months later on the resale, thus providing the agent with double fees. An owner-occupier will not do that, and is therefore effectively discriminated against by the private treaty agent.

No such discrimination exists in the auction room. Any buyer, whatever his colour, race or creed, has the same chance as the next man of buying what he wants, provided he is prepared to pay the market price for it. There are few real bargains to be had at auction these days – they are far too popular – but at least they provide all the attendees with a fair chance of securing what they have set out to buy (and one or two auctioneering firms are providing a panoply of financial services to help them, these including accountants and solicitors in the sale room).

As residential investment stocks dwindle, so it seems to be replaced by residential vacant houses and flats, in which it is felt there is potential for auction growth. Several hitherto commercial-only firms of auctioneers have been tempted to cross the traditional line that once divided residential and commercial auctions, and have started a residential side in anticipation of this new source of instruction. Other auction firms have been going in the opposite direction, from residential to commercial but perhaps with less success.

The average lot size sold at auction has increased by fifty per cent in recent years but from 1985–6 it went up a hundredfold, with some firms reporting an increase from £200,000-300,000, in their average lot size, during 1986. The psychological barrier, that once excluded lots of £1 million or over, seems to have been broken and buyers are regularly seen happily bidding that amount and more at the larger sales. As a consequence, sales turnover has increased dramati-

◆ INTRODUCTION ◆

cally. For example, one firm reported figures of £13.519 million for 1981 and £105 million for 1986. Individual sales have increased in terms of the number of lots offered. Another firm's figures are illustrative: it offered 273 lots in 1981 and 549 in 1986; it achieved £1 million per sale in 1981 and £33 million per sale in 1986.

Figures produced by the London Auction Mart for sales conducted under their roof show an increase in lots offered from 2972 in 1984 to 6478 in 1986, while the total value of their sales went up from £81.48 million in 1984, to £209.17 million in 1986. In 1983 and 1984, the *Chartered Surveyor Weekly* compiled league tables which defined the most successful firm as the one with the greatest turnover. However, this is not the only factor contributing to a successful auctioneer. It is also his 'percentage sold' rate that should be taken into account when assessing who is best for a certain property. Some firms have been known to take on any property, whether it would sell or not, simply to pad out their catalogue and to produce a packed house on the day. Some will also quote unrealistic guide prices to potential buyers, and inflated reserves to potential sellers in the hope of getting instructions. The same practice is also found in the private treaty market as a growing number of agents compete for a more or less finite number of potential vendors.

An auctioneer is only as good as his last sale. A success rate of ninety per cent or over is considered very good, under seventy per cent is not impressive. So what makes a good auctioneer? There is no official training for the position, although most leading auctioneers are Chartered Surveyors and will insist that their reserve auctioneers and assistants are similarly qualified. Most of the leading auctioneers have fallen into the job by chance rather than choice, usually on the death or retirement of the existing auctioneer. None of them actually set out to become one.

What an auctioneer needs, however, is to be part-actor, part-showman, with a good clear voice and a comprehensive command of the English language. He must be able to hold

♦ INTRODUCTION ♦

an audience of several hundred people for up to eight hours and be able to deal with difficult and obstinate customers, without appearing rude and unhelpful. He must have a presence on the rostrum and be able to control the sale from start to finish. Tact and diplomacy come high on the list of qualifications since today's buyers could become tomorrow's sellers and end up as the auctioneer's clients if he impresses his skills upon them.

Many agents may be attracted to the auction world by the huge profits they see the major firms making, but they are undoubtedly deterred by the costs involved in staging such an auction. These will be into six figures: just to post 10,000 catalogues will cost over £20,000, not to mention the production and printing costs (at least one auction house is trying to offset some of these costs by accepting selected advertising in the catalogue). Added to this is the hire of the room, plus tea and refreshments for the attendees, advertising (another £20,000 or so), staff and other miscellaneous expenses. It is no wonder that agents who have suitable auction properties, but not enough of them perhaps to stage their own sale, generally prefer to give them to the large established firms of auctioneers, thus saving themselves the cost of holding their own auction, and giving them the benefit of a moiety of the auctioneer's commission.

♦

As can be seen from the foregoing, the auction side of surveying practice has become more significant as a source of revenue to agents and surveyors, and auctions are also increasingly seen by clients as a viable means of realising value quickly. The organisation of auctions and their relationship to the surveying practices and the property professional's activities have become more complex and structured than ever before.

The present book covers all aspects of modern professional property auctioneering practice. It outlines the background to the business, the types of property sold at auction, the qualifications and aptitudes of auctioneers, his legal duties

♦ INTRODUCTION ♦

and the organisation that makes auctioneering a successful enterprise. It is intended not only for practising and aspiring surveyors and auctioneers, but also for vendors and purchasers of property at auction, from the large company to the man-in-the-street, to provide information for those who regularly use or would like to use auctions to acquire or dispose of property. The book will allow existing auctioneers to increase their professionalism and give the buyer of their services greater knowledge and appreciation of what he is purchasing.

All the contributors (with the exception of the last) are professional auctioneers of many years' standing.

• I •

The Auction Department and the Auctioneer

Tony Trump FRICS, *of Edward Erdman*

The structure of an auction department is just the same as for any other business, whether it is concerned with auctioning property, assessing pineapple markets or advertising penny dreadfuls. An auction calls for opportunity, instruction, inspection, law, research, marketing, administration, finance and staffing. There is no real difference from the selling of any other product, if the word 'inspection' is omitted from that short list.

We need to examine all these commonplace activities in some detail as, by appreciating their implications, the structure of an auction department takes shape. The headings are largely in chronological order. There is some blurring of the edges between them and a great deal of overlap caused by having many lots, several clients and up to four sales in the course of execution or preparation at any one time.

Finally, there is the auctioneer himself. Part actor, part agent, part lawyer, sometimes admired, occasionally hated, often the topic of conversation, he occupies what to him can seem the loneliest place on earth.

Opportunity

The auction market is a lively and healthy one and therefore changing constantly. The lot sold yesterday may not sell today and today's unsuitable property may be the fashion of tomorrow. Evidence of this in the London area, for example, has been the enormous increase in the sale by auction of vacant (usually Victorian) houses over the past five years; whereas previously it was residential investments that were primarily offered. House owners have seemingly grown confident enough to become their own developers and have taken advantage of the many sources of finance readily available. In addition, as the private (and now public) landlord has declined, the auction houses that made a living from such purchasers and vendors have switched to promoting the sale by auction of vacant houses in poor condition and thus replacing – for the auctioneer – the ever-dwindling stock of residential investments.

Similarly, in the commercial field, prime vacant and investment properties were frequently offered by auction in the early 1970s but were subsequently withdrawn from the auction market. Auctioneers are now 'experimenting' with such property again, as are owners, and they have succeeded in re-establishing its place in the auction room. The renewed popularity of commercial property auctions is such that one may expect to find good property being offered, and sold at figures equivalent to or better than might be anticipated in a private negotiation.

As the market alters, the auctioneer has to detect those changes so that, as opportunities to sell properties arise, a client can be accurately advised on the most prudent form of disposal, be it private treaty, auction or formal tender, the latter also regaining importance. It used to be said that if the value of a property was fairly certain it should be offered by private treaty, if the value was in some doubt, by auction, and if the competition was sufficiently great and the value uncertain that the property should be put to tender. To a certain extent these criteria still hold true but currently an auction may be expected to include properties which, hitherto, would have been sold by one of the other means available, the auction having then been considered the last resort. Vendors are now sensitive to the strong auction climate which has revitalised the market considerably by attracting buyers to auctions who are willing to pay good

◆ THE AUCTION DEPARTMENT ◆

prices for properties which are 'freshly for sale'. Gone are the days when 'last-ditch properties' purchased by property morticians, with yields barely exceeding financing rates, were virtually all that were offered.

The auctioneer's function as far as both vendor and purchaser are concerned is to assess the constantly changing climate. As new types of property become successfully saleable by auction so new types of disposal methods also arise, sometimes from force of circumstances, sometimes from an intuition of what can or will succeed. For instance, transatlantic auctions for property have taken place as have videolinked auctions within the U.K., joining bidders in two separate auction rooms; at least three practices have ventured into holding sales of property in Scotland and into tendering properties on short leases. Some of these efforts to provide another weapon in the armoury of disposal means have been very successful, others less so.

Instruction

In any particular area of the market there are several auctioneers practising, offering differing services and costs and a wide variety of potential sale dates. A first-time vendor at auction, with no experience of the firms who offer an auction service, will initially only be conscious of what the various auctioneers' catalogues look like; from these he will be able to assess the types of property in which the various auctioneers normally specialise.

The auctioneer himself may have no knowledge of this preliminary scrutiny which may or may not result in work being offered. But, thereafter, all the normal ways of attracting a potential client to one's own service come into play: speed and quality of service, competitive fees, low costs, efficiency, credibility and understanding of the 'problem', to name but a few. Of the properties which come into the auctioneer's sights, there will be a high fall-out rate, not least because the 'vendor' may only have been drawn in originally by the prospect of a free valuation. But given that some firms hold monthly sales of as many as eighty properties, for eight or nine months of the year, while some have a sale occasionally with an unpredictable number of lots, and others, half a dozen sales a year each with about twenty to twenty-five lots, the auctioneer may at any one time be processing from initial consideration through to completion of sale, eighty to a hundred properties, all of which actually appear in the catalogue – i.e. are not 'failures'. The larger auction houses will handle ten to twenty times this number of lots.

Inspection

Sometimes a property may be cursorily inspected at an early stage to give an estimate of realisation. But the main inspection for cataloguing will involve detailed measurement; checking of boundaries (and, in the case of let and, particularly, multi-let property, ensuring that the boundaries of the lettings encompass the areas expected, and that there has been no apparent encroachment into or over the property), logical easement runs for drainage, cables, and the like, rights of way (vehicle and foot), flying freeholds, extensions and improvements (Are they the tenant's? If so, they are probably not part of the property to be described in the particulars of sale), state of repair, statutory notices concerning pedestrianisation, compulsory purchase and dangerous structures and a host of other factors. Not to be forgotten is information – such as special possible purchasers – which is more easily collected on the spot and which will assist later at the marketing stage, when a snippet or two of local 'interest', can stimulate otherwise lethargic bidding, if judiciously timed.

Law

The parcel of legal documents containing office copy entries, filed plans, leases, licences, searches, pre-contract and general tenancy enquiries, will ideally be to hand (and seldom is) at the time of inspection. Prior, careful examination of these not only makes the inspection itself easier but also more useful. It is so much simpler to check a property against the

♦ THE AUCTION DEPARTMENT ♦

documents than it is to assess the degree to which a property accords with the documents later, in the office, against photographs of dustbins, rain-sodden notebooks written with numb fingers holding on to many other bits and pieces, and the weakness of memory. However, ascertaining whether the property and the legal documents are in accord is one thing; being sure one has all the documents is another, as is detecting whether clauses required by current conveyancing practice (but often not at the time the sometimes very old documents were drawn up) are missing.

Sadly, not all solicitors are at home with what the auctioneer needs, or appreciate the reasonableness of his screams of urgency.

Valuation

To sell a property by auction, just as by other means of disposal, requires much research into evidence of value, as well as the intuitive skills of the valuer. The auctioneer must know what a property is likely to fetch in order to advise on the reserve. As there is little difference in the techniques applied in this valuation to any other, there is no great merit in reiterating much of what will be already understood or can be learned elsewhere by the reader. Later chapters detail some of the particular problems of fixing the reserve price.

Marketing

One word, with enormous implications. Marketing ranges from the practical placement of a small advertisement in a suitable newspaper or journal through the accuracy of mailing lists, appearance and layout of catalogue and telephone manner, to the way in which an auctioneer is known to conduct his business – his credibility.

A host of people and bodies must be contacted in a variety of ways, each tailored to the particular recipient: tenants, agents, dealers, retailers, accountants, contractors, occupiers, landowners, architects – the list seems endless, but since any one could produce the most enthusiastic purchaser, all need attention. Just as a linage advertisement is not the way for a property to be brought to the attention of someone who owns a portfolio of property in the subject area and with whom you have previously concluded business, so a mail-shot to all householders within fifty yards or miles would seem inapposite.

Where auctions may differ from other kinds of disposal is in appealing sometimes to buyers who would not contemplate negotiation by private treaty, for instance, the overseas buyer who may have scant knowledge of the language not to mention the legal aspects of making a purchase. This is a difficult field to explore and to reach by marketing, but it is one of increasing importance for some types of property.

Administration and Finance

To avoid endless script, two examples of check-lists are reproduced (see facing page and Appendix 6), showing various aspects of the work of an auction department and emphasising that short cuts are dangerous in most instances, disastrous in some.

In addition to the detailed checking needed for each individual lot in the printer's proofs (at the two to five proof stages) there is a great deal to be organised in the context of the room and the auction itself. To name some of the things that have to be attended to (but which are not always obvious and easy to forget):

1. to book the hall with microphones, recording equipment, telephones, catering, seating plan and rostrum layout;
2. to transport to the auction room, direction boards, message boards, messengers, gavel (!), auctioneer's identity board, Acts of Parliament for display, spare catalogues, copies of the addenda and document packages for each lot;
3. to check security in the room and to arrange for the banking of deposits, to send contracts to the solicitors, to inform vendors and the press and any record systems that are kept by the partnership or company of the results and last, and by no means least, to check all the accounts from suppliers and to pay them promptly.

◆ THE AUCTION DEPARTMENT ◆
CHECK-LIST OF ESSENTIAL ACTIVITIES FOR A SINGLE PROPERTY

Any joint agency? Terms?
Terms of appointment sent
Signed terms of appointment returned

Solicitor's instructions sent
Solicitor's instructions acknowledged
Appointments for survey made

Keys/Orders to view to hand
O. S./Goad to hand

Survey concluded
Queries to solicitor sent
Suitable photos to hand

O. S./Goad update done
Particulars drafted
Queries to solicitors answered

Boards ordered
Special Conditions – draft to hand
Identity all occupiers/keys, etc.

Proofs of particulars ex printer
– to client
– to solicitor
– corrected by auctioneer
– corrected by client

– corrected by solicitor
– full corrections to printer
Lotting order
Necessary documents to hand?
Notify all occupiers

Document package made up

Mailshot

Draft addenda
Draft addenda approved by auctioneer
– corrected by solicitor
1st addenda printed

Appointments to fix reserves
Fix reserves

Sale

In-house instructions to departments
'Sold by' board overlays

A/cs and expenses drafted
Completion statement drafted
Letter to client
Letter to solicitor

Remove all 'Sold by' boards

A/cs paid

Firms operate differently in the way they service auction work; some have surveyors dealing almost exclusively with auction work, others use surveying skills deployed in the firm to service auction and other needs.

Another area of divergence between practices is the level of financial self-sufficiency expected of the auction department. For some practices, notably the larger agency-oriented ones, it is almost essential nowadays to be seen to be auctioneers. To provide that service, in the formative years at least, the firm will have to tolerate losses from auction work, anticipating a profit centre developing in the wake of the investment. In some firms of long standing with successful auction departments, it would seem that the auction itself is a substantial creator of positive cashflow.

Firms differ in the way they charge fees and expenses to the client. Some prefer to charge a fixed sum to vendors on the win-some-lose-some principle, others account strictly for expenses incurred, some even charge for the 'management' of those expenses. Some auctioneers charge expenses at the time of taking instructions, thus further assisting cashflow – a sometimes necessary precaution against subsequent expensive delay or the occasional disreputable vendor.

Whatever method of subsidising or charging is adopted, there are numerous overheads and payments to suppliers (for example, printers, signwriters, advertisers, caterers, venue owners) whose co-operation is vital to an efficient and successful auction department.

Deposits are held on behalf of vendors – some auctioneers hold as agents, some as stakeholders – lodged in client accounts and payable to the correct body in the fullness of legal time. Property auctioneers are generally permitted to deduct their fees and expenses from the deposit, a feature which could be looked upon with some envy by their fellows in other sectors. This reduces, though only reduces, the degree to which an auctioneer, when compared with those selling property by other means, acts as banker to his client.

The management of these interrelated financial matters has

◆ THE AUCTION DEPARTMENT ◆

been significantly eased by the relatively cheap availability of the ubiquitous chip.

Computers and Administration

An administrative aid in running property auctions is the computer which can both save on staff and increase efficiency.

Microcomputers, using word-processing and database programmes, can handle, maintain and adapt mailing lists, assist in drafting particulars and in sending out standardised letters of instructions to clients, solicitors and joint auctioneers, can update checklists and help with general correspondence with owners, vendors and purchasers. The computer can speed up communication with the press, advertising media and public relations specialists, printers, venue organisers and other suppliers. They can also be useful internally, in analysing results, and in accounting.

The accounts are extremely complex in that all costs incurred, whether they be for travelling, room hire, hotels, printing, boards, photographs or whatever, are expenses borne in differing amounts by various clients but usually recovered according to the amount of space a lot takes in a catalogue. To complicate matters further, in some cases, certain costs are met by the firm, while for lots sold before or after a sale, rather than during, fees may be levied on a sliding scale.

Inputting all this information and the basis of calculation for each, produces not only accounts but a complete analysis of costs incurred by the auctioneer per lot for differing types of property in different areas and the costs for differing sizes of sales and properties. It also provides reliable information on prices achieved against reserves, and on a host of other facts which ensure a more reliable service to clients and tightens internal cost control.

Another task more easily accomplished by computer is the preparation of the draft catalogue for a sale so that it can then be transferred electronically to the printer's production equipment. This not only saves much time but reduces costs and eliminates many printer's errors.

Staffing

Mention has already been made of the different ways in which practices view their own auction activity, either as unavoidable or as a primary force in terms of both practicality and finance. Clearly the structure of the department will depend upon these viewpoints and will be a blend of determination, quality of staff available and expediency.

The conduct of auction work is so complex and its different facets so interrelated that to 'sub-contract' elements of the work to non-auction personnel is an expedient to be avoided – and where necessitated, by sickness say, can be more of a hindrance than an assistance. The disadvantages of the auction-only department are far outweighed by the advantages which can be summarised in the words, cohesion, understanding, responsibility and dedication. The single responsibility which the members of department hold means that each is aware not only of what is happening and can therefore cover fairly effectively when needed, but also of the urgency of careful dovetailing of all the activities, not to mention the consequences of failing at any point.

It is a good principle to have all properties inspected fully by two people simultaneously, a qualified senior and a qualified junior, and to make all the subsequent functions relating to that property, the province of those two people. Such a utopian state of affairs is always fragile since sickness, holidays and other factors necessitate flexibility, but continuity can be achieved by an overlap between the teams of two.

However, as the department expands, the teams will change and the intended staffing level will rarely take account of the unexpected twists of opportunity, while individuals may mature faster, or slower, than anticipated. In any event, the basic concept of a team of two dealing with all aspects of the progress of a particular property has much to commend it, not least that there is always an element of

♦ THE AUCTION DEPARTMENT ♦

knowledge stored in the head and, by continuity, the risks of incorrect interpretation or pure lack of awareness do not arise in passing a 'job' from one team to another.

This degree of manpower is, however, beyond the resources or commitment of some practices and not within the business plan of others. For those conducting the occasional sale, the short term deployment of certain competent staff to the forthcoming auction has obvious attractions and the quantity and type of lots to be sold will determine the number and calibre of staff and the amount of attention required. Equally, an auction which is simply the product of client demand, rather than the result of a positive decision to enter the field, may be developed by existing staff in various divisions of the firm attending to different aspects of the work and co-ordinating their effort as efficiently as possible, rather than created anew. Colleague auctioneers who work in this way encounter the inevitable problems that can arise in busy organisations where the job for the partner with the loudest voice (not always that of the auctioneer) gets priority. For the auctioneer, with critical time constraints, that can be, at the very least, inconvenient.

A surveyor who is competent to handle all aspects of auction work is a rare being, professional but entrepreneurial, extrovert but painstaking and methodical, able to operate under considerable pressure from colleagues, clients, printers and solicitors, simultaneously, and a solo performer to boot! Few people exhibit such breadth of talent, once described in a provocative advertisement for a new vacancy in an auction department as the 'Ultimate Surveyor'.

Finally, a word of warning to anyone contemplating taking on auction work. The time-consuming nature of the task must not be underestimated, since cutting corners, by leaving a fair bit up to the client or his solicitors or the joint auctioneer, could expose partner and practice alike to heavy legal costs. To vary the adage a little, 'they will get what the "client" pays for,' and if they offer an unsubsidised cheaper service to their clients, they may find that they get it in the neck from lawyers; the cost of negligence cover these days, as all professionals are only too aware, is high.

The Auctioneer

Most people are somewhat intrigued by what possible type of person the auctioneer can be.

As pointed out in the Introduction, he clearly has to be something of a showman, to stand up in public and make a verbal, and sometimes physical, display of himself. Styles vary from the restrained and dignified demeanour of the elegantly dressed, self-assured professional London auctioneer to the flamboyant figure who addresses massively overcrowded rooms of scruffy purchasers, many of whom would not appear to be able to muster the proverbial brass farthings, in small provincial towns. Some auctioneers say little on the rostrum, some keep up an endless patter to enliven the proceedings, some coax the bids, some almost batter them out of would-be buyers − all are performers. But there is one great difference between an auctioneer and most other public performers: the audience is there not to assist him but to take as much advantage of him as possible, while he is there as the arbiter of what they can, for their own benefit, get away with.

Behind the public persona, the auctioneer must be pleasant to all, must command authority and be articulate with his presentation. He needs also to be in keeping with the grade of property offered. He must have a good working knowledge of auction law, must be decisive and, when in trouble, exude confidence. Above all, he must retain a good sense of humour in times of crisis, be an efficient administrator and able to create an atmosphere of dedication to succeed amongst his colleagues − who must all be fighting against time, the auctioneer's greatest enemy.

The Multi-Department Practice and the Sole Auctioneer

Despite the long history of the auction, outside London there are few firms who could fairly be considered as regular conductors of auctions of property, and fewer still who

◆ THE AUCTION DEPARTMENT ◆

specifically handle commercial property by this means (in other words who schedule regular multi-lot auctions as opposed to conducting an auction only when events dictate). The vast proportion of commercial property put to auction in the United Kingdom is handled by London firms who hold sales at central locations in the capital.

There is, therefore, small opportunity for the sole auctioneer to function. On the other hand, there are some highly respected firms whose reputation is chiefly based on their auction business and who have progressed from the residential to the commercial auction sphere. Historically, such firms coupled their auction business with substantial residential or residentially-biased management work. They have been joined over the last few years by a growing number of practices who have added auctions to their 'services available'. The point has now been reached where there is no such thing as an 'auction house', such as exists in the chattels field. All firms conducting auction business do it as a part of their overall operation.

Whilst comparative figures are not available it seems likely that for some the auction activity contributes a significant proportion of turnover, while for others the auction function may produce a smaller proportion of overall profitability, as the profit per head on auction work is low in comparison with, for instance, financial or development consultancy. In consequence, if the auction market were to ail, one would expect to find firms in the latter group withdrawing from auctions and redeploying personnel to other more profitable fields. In the event, it is likely that sales for all would diminish in size or frequency: few firms would cease to conduct auctions completely.

There is no doubt that, whatever type of firm practises in auctions, it is a very visible activity and a firm as a whole is affected by the conduct of its auction activities. In recent years, auctions, though principally chattel auctions, have become an area of media and, therefore, public interest. Because of the high profile of auctions and the large turnover of some auction houses, it is assumed that all,

◆ PROPERTY AUCTIONS ◆

proportionately, do as well and charge the same rates for their service. Yet the profit margins for property auctioneering are slim by comparison with high value works of art: the buyer's premium does not exist and vendor's fees are relatively minute. But public perception is different, and an area perceived as a potential goldmine will attract interest from those wishing to enter the field.

What lies ahead in the book, while exploding some of these myths, may encourage those who thought property auctions inappropriate to their transactions, or their means, to try buying or selling through them.

♦ 2 ♦

Auction Preparation and Presentation

John Barnett FRICS, *of Harman Healy*

ASSEMBLING THE AUCTION

The Date of the Auction

It might seem to the vendor that the simplest part of arranging an auction is to fix the date and book the venue, but even this initial step needs careful consideration. Most London auctioneers, for instance, meet early in January under the umbrella of the London Auction Mart to plan the auction dates for the coming year, primarily to avoid clashing with each other. Certain days, such as religious holidays, Fridays, bank holidays, and popular holiday periods, like the end of July and the whole of August, need to be avoided; also the State Opening of Parliament and general elections, if known about in time. Some auctioneers try not to hold sales in December, January or most of February, but with the popularity of the auction route, this appears impossible for most auction houses nowadays.

Venue

The auctioneer has to produce the right atmosphere at an auction and thus the choice of room is important. For some years, many of the regular auctions have been held under the auspices of the London Auction Mart at the Connaught Rooms in Holborn, where there is a variety of room sizes with seating capacities ranging from thirty-five to a thousand persons. For a possible attendance of a hundred and fifty the room should have a seating capacity of about a hundred and twenty-five, plus some spare chairs stacked up. There is far more atmosphere in a full room than in one with empty seats.

A London auction is best timed so that the sale does not finish too late, as buyers may not be keen to stay on after dark or to confront the rush hour. It is not uncommon for a larger auction sale to start at one o'clock or to be held in two sessions, commencing at eleven o'clock, with an hour's break for lunch, and sometimes a short afternoon break for tea. Refreshments provided by the auctioneer encourage bidders to arrive on time!

In the case of the occasional auction, where a firm recommends holding an auction perhaps for a single property, and it is not likely to attract the London investment market, the auctioneer will probably suggest holding the auction locally in a well-known hotel or public house, with a starting time in the early evening, when there will be a greater chance of a large local turnout. As well as drumming up more interest in the property, the auctioneer may well gain new business for himself.

Lead Times and Co-Ordination

The auctioneer will aim to have the printed catalogue ready at least four weeks before the sale date, in order that potential purchasers may have sufficient (but not too much) time to make inspections, surveys and other inquiries, before the day of the sale. Typesetting, proofing and printing the catalogue will take about six weeks, so some eight to ten weeks will be needed to prepare the sale adequately. The accompanying check-list shows the threads that have to be tied together by the auction department before the catalogue is sent to press, while the check-list shown in Appendix 6 gives a step-by-step account of the procedures necessary to ensure that the catalogue proofs are correct. The importance of producing an accurate catalogue is discussed further below (p. 21).

♦ AUCTION PREPARATION ♦

CATALOGUE PREPARATION CHECK-LIST

	10 weeks	8 weeks	6 weeks
Instructions received	√		
Instructions confirmed	√		
Solicitors instructed	√		
Documents received		√	
Special Conditions received		√	
Inspected		√	
Photograph ordered/taken		√	
Photograph received		√	
Details done		√	
Proof to client		√	
Proof to printer		√	
Proof corrected			√
Corrections to printer			√
Special Conditions to printer			√
Keys to office			√
Write to tenant			√
Order board			√
Board up			√

◆ PROPERTY AUCTIONS ◆

The Agreement between Vendor and Auctioneer

The terms that are agreed between vendor and auctioneer have nowadays to be comprehensive and in accordance with the Estate Agents Act 1979 (see Appendix). They ought to be in writing, and signed by both parties, who will each retain a copy.

These terms refer to the fees to be charged and the amount earmarked for expenses. The former may range from one to five per cent, depending on the size of the lot, and the latter from £100-1,000 depending on the space taken in the catalogue and whether it is printed in black and white or colour. Expenses may be requested or even demanded in advance. The following extracts from a typical contract show the main areas that are laid down between vendor and the auctioneer; as new situations occur revisions and additions may become necessary.

. . . 3. Instructions to submit the above-mentioned property for sale by way of public auction are accepted subject to the following:

(i) The sale commission shall be . . .% + VAT of the Sale Price

(ii) The Vendor's contribution towards the auction expenses shall be £. . . + VAT

. . . 5. In addition to the commission payable the Vendor will be responsible for a contribution towards the Auction Costs as specified above being the Vendor's contribution towards the cost of printing of the auction particulars, advertising, etc. In the event that the Vendor shall fail to pay the said sum (plus VAT) within 7 days of written demand in that behalf made by the Auctioneers then the Auctioneers reserve the right to withdraw the property from the auction and the Vendor shall have no claim against the auctioneers. The Vendor shall still remain liable to pay the said sum (plus VAT).

. . . 7. If the property is withdrawn by the Vendor (other

◆ AUCTION PREPARATION ◆

than by reason of a sale before the auction) between the date of the Vendor's instructions and the auction the Vendor shall pay commission at the rate of one half of the commission which would have been payable on a sale at the reserve price (if already notified to the Auctioneers) or at a price determined by the Auctioneers (in their absolute discretion) as representing a reserve price in the event that a reserve price had not been so notified to the auctioneers.

. . . 11. The Auctioneers shall hold the deposit as agents for the Vendor. The Auctioneer shall account to the Vendor or the Vendor's solicitor for the deposits less fees and expenses as soon as practicable after the date of the auction sale even though completion may not have taken place.

. . . 12. The Auctioneers shall have complete discretion as to whether a purchaser's cheque shall be accepted or refused for the deposit and whether or not to require such deposit to be paid by way of Banker's Draft or cash.

. . . 14. The Auctioneers are instructed to bid on behalf of the Vendor at their discretion up to the reserve and to regulate the bidding. The Vendor shall not bid for the property nor shall any agent so bid on his behalf. In the event that the sale of the property shall be set aside through breach of this condition by the Vendor or his agent then the Vendor shall nevertheless be responsible for the commission as set out in Clause 3 at the price at which the property was knocked down together with the costs and VAT payable pursuant to Clause 3.

The Vendor must not bid the reserve price or higher but should the property be 'bought in' by the Vendor or his agent whether inadvertently or not, twice the agreed commission as specified in Clause 3 will be payable.

. . . 16. In the event of a dispute between bidders the Auctioneer is authorised to determine the dispute or to resubmit the property at his sole discretion.

◆ PROPERTY AUCTIONS ◆

As a further protection, some firms now include a clause, when dealing with new and unknown corporate clients (especially if registered overseas), making the directors personally liable to them for the fees and expenses, since it is not unusual for the deposit to be paid direct to the vendor's solicitors on a sale either prior to or after auction, thus requiring the auctioneer to submit his account and hope for a settlement.

The Conditions of Sale, which apply to all lots, also need frequent revision in the light of new experience. Nearly all London auctioneers currently use the National Conditions of Sale (20th edition) or a modified version of them (see Appendix), as they are considered more favourable to vendors, despite allowing assignment of contracts and sub-sales, than the Law Society's General Conditions of Sale (1984 Revision).

Contact with the Vendor's Solicitors

The vendor's solicitors should hear from the auctioneers with a request for the following:

1. Special Conditions of Sale (kept to a minimum) which have regard to the standard general Conditions of Sale provided by the auctioneer.
2. Copies of the leases, licences, agreements and any other documents referred to in the Special Conditions and Particulars of Sale.
3. Office copy entries and filed plans for registered land or equivalent documents if the land is unregistered.
4. An up-to-date local search in readiness for the auction. This usually takes four to six weeks to arrive but is essential for many purchasers before they buy especially if they require a mortgage.

The auction department needs to check its inspection notes of the property on receipt of these documents to ensure they correspond with the title deeds and the tenancy particulars.

◆ AUCTION PREPARATION ◆

The latter should be made available to prospective purchasers and/or their solicitors.

Property Inspection and Preparation of Particulars

In the last twenty years, the weight of the law generally has shifted from favouring the seller to protecting the buyer. In the property field, while an estate agent who puts out misleading particulars in marketing a property for sale by private treaty can only be sued for misrepresentation, and may indeed be covered by the disclaimer printed at the bottom of the particulars, the auctioneer who publishes incorrect information in his catalogue can, because the catalogue itself forms part of the contract of sale, with the memorandum of agreement physically bound in at the back, be sued for negligence. The auctioneer cannot rely on printing a disclaimer in the catalogue.

Misdescription, to the extent that something purchased is materially different from what the purchaser believes he is buying, was considered to override any disclaimers made by auctioneers in the nineteenth century case of *Flight v Booth* (1834) 1 Bing NC 370. The principle was upheld more recently in the case of *King Brothers (Finance) Ltd v North Western British Road Services Ltd* [1986] 2 EGLR 253, where the auction catalogue overestimated the square footage of office space being sold.

Even a slight mistake on the auctioneer's part in the particulars of sale may be sufficient for a purchaser to be able to negotiate a reduction of the price after exchange. The auctioneer must be equally cautious with information communicated verbally (for a fuller discussion of this, see below, chapter 9).

With this in mind, the auctioneer's inspection should be carried out by at least one surveyor (see previous chapter), who will check the basement, rear access, rights of way, flying freeholds, and other matters that need accurate description. He must for instance be very careful if he calls a room an 'office', not to imply, if it is not the case, that there is consent for office use.

♦ PROPERTY AUCTIONS ♦

Sometimes, where an investment property is being sold, the lessees will not permit inspection of the property because, for example, the lease states that this can only be done in the case of inspecting the condition of the building and a Schedule of Dilapidations has already been complied with. It has to be made clear that no inspection has been made by the auctioneer and that the accommodation has only been estimated in the particulars.

The auctioneer will have to read the lease – it is not enough for him to know the rent revision is in 1990, if it is only to fifty per cent of the market value. He needs to be very precise as to the identity of commercial tenants. For example, a company may be a subsidiary of a large public company, but not guaranteed by them, thus any reference to the parent company must not imply that they are the lessees. If the lease is a full repairing one, it may still have a Schedule of Condition attached, to which the auctioneer should refer.

In the case of residential tenancies, the full initials of the tenant should be stated but not, according to an RICS requirement, the tenant's sex. The auctioneer will also want a copy of the rent registration to indicate when the next one is due.

The particulars should be set out clearly, preferably in separate headed columns as here (see also Appendix 3):

LOT NO.	PROPERTY	TENANT & TRADE	TERM	ANN. EX. RENTAL	REMARKS
8	10 High St.	Mr & Mrs Smith Ladies' Hairdressers	20 yrs from 1/3/87	£2,000	5 yearly reviews

The plan and photograph should be incorporated with the particulars, rather than grouped elsewhere in the catalogue, to help avoid errors on the part of bidders. It is useful to have the telephone number of the local planning office, and the relevant extension number included, if the property has any redevelopment potential. If the property is vacant there

♦ AUCTION PREPARATION ♦

must be indications of how it can be inspected and where the keys may be obtained for access.

Both vendor and auctioneer need to be aware of their duty under the Occupiers Liability Act 1957 to visitors to their premises. If these are derelict or potentially dangerous, prospective purchasers should be warned in the particulars, and must not be permitted to make an inspection without an appointment.

Finally, if the vendor has joint auctioneers acting for him, the second auctioneer's details, including references, should appear in the particulars.

Guide Prices

No prices are printed in the catalogue (although one firm has taken to giving some guide prices) but before it is distributed an approximate reserve price has to be agreed between the vendor and auctioneer, as an indication for prospective buyers; and the vendor has to decide at what price, if any, he will sell prior to auction. From this information, the auction department prepares a guide that may range from below the reserve to the 'sell-prior' figure. This will enable it to give an immediate response to prospective purchasers; some firms will sell fifteen to thirty per cent of lots prior to auction. In the case of poorer lots, if an offer is received before the auction, an auctioneer may recommend acceptance if he feels the offer might not be repeated in the auction room and that the property is unlikely to attract other bids from the floor.

Advertising and Public Relations

The auctioneer has four main forms of advertising at his disposal: the press, radio and television; 'for sale' boards; mailing lists; and personal promotion.

The Press Auctions are mainly advertised in the established property journals, namely, the weekly *Estates Gazette* which has a very extensive readership and concentrates auction advertisements and auction news in one section, and the

◆ PROPERTY AUCTIONS ◆

Chartered Surveyor Weekly, which is sent to all RICS members (and non-members on subscription), and gives considerable coverage to auctions. The national press, *The Times*, the *Daily Telegraph*, and the *London Evening Standard*, for instance, have a much larger circulation but are relatively expensive pro rata and despite their property sections are not well-known for auctions. Local papers, on the other hand, are cheap to advertise in, and have been found useful outside London for attracting buyers who may have money to invest but have thought the property field was too difficult to enter.

Radio and Television Given an unusual or famous property to sell, the auctioneer will generally employ a public relations expert to promote the sale and capture public interest. In some cases, such a sale will be worthy of the attention of the national news. Considerable publicity from this source has been given to sales of Scottish islands, tin mines, ice houses, even to the auction of the narrowest house in London.

'For Sale' Boards Whilst these are the norm for estate agents, auctioneers find them of limited use except possibly for vacant property, and sites and investments where local interest may be generated. A board on an investment in, say, Oxford Street will not generally attract attention whereas a shop investment in a country town may well be noticed by wealthy locals. Many auctioneers order boards to be erected without permission from the tenants and the display of the words 'Business not affected' is intended to allay the tenant's fears. But it is very rare for a lease to provide that the freeholders can erect a board, and the government, in the face of proliferating boards, is subjecting them to control for residential property.

Mailing Lists The auctioneer's mailing list is a valuable tool from which the vendor will benefit. Such a list may contain several thousand names and, with a computer, can be kept up to date. It is built up from the response to advertising and from reports of auction sales in the property press; if the

♦ AUCTION PREPARATION ♦

auctioneer's firm has a private treaty investment department, appropriate names may be culled from it. From the auctioneer's point of view, a good mailing list encourages likely purchasers to become vendors and to instruct the auctioneer to include their properties in future auctions.

Personal Promotion The auctioneer is only too aware that his ability on the rostrum is a factor which helps attract or discourage future clients. While a good speaking voice may be an advantage for some sorts of sales, much more important to vendor and prospective purchaser alike is the auctioneer's handling of the many questions that may be put to him at any time before and during the bidding. He has to have a thorough knowledge of Landlord and Tenant Acts, Rent Acts, planning, management, building construction, lease terminology, conditions of sale, the law of contract and other matters on which bidders are entitled to be informed. The auctioneer is, however, aided and abetted by other experts from his office and solicitors who may deal with more specialist questions, and in the event of such a question the auctioneer will invite the enquirer up to the rostrum to discuss it with the appropriate person.

AT THE SALE

Staff

The auctioneer will almost always have a reserve or assistant auctioneer who can take over the entire sale in an emergency and who will have been given frequent opportunities on the rostrum to gain experience. It has, incidentally, been known for firms to charge a different scale of fees according to which auctioneer has dealt with a particular lot.

The auctioneer will also have a 'spotter' who stands next to him and looks at the parts of the room the auctioneer is not himself covering at any particular time. The auctioneer, not wishing to take his eye off the bidder when he is in the process of knocking down a lot, relies on the spotter to notice the under-bidder trying to bid at the last moment.

◆ PROPERTY AUCTIONS ◆

There will also be two or three 'runners', who will stand on the auction platform, facing the room, so that they can see to whom the auctioneer is selling, and, following the final bid, will approach the buyer immediately, with a card, to obtain name and address and, if possible, a deposit cheque. It has been found to be wisest to obtain the cheque at this point rather than to wait for the buyer to reappear at the end of the sale.

Two senior persons should handle the completion of the memoranda and their exchange. Normally, no change of purchaser's name from that on the original card is permitted since the card identifies the bidder and it is he who is liable under the contract made at the fall of the hammer.

There will probably be someone present to enter the cheques directly into a paying-in book so that they can be sent round to the bank. A bank will, by prior arrangement, accept cheques up to four o'clock and will send them off the same evening for special clearance. Thus, the auction department usually knows by the next morning whether or not the deposit cheques have cleared. At major London auctions, where deposits for very large lots are drawn on London banks, the cheques are paid in directly to the drawer's bank so that instant clearance is obtained.

Methods of Bidding

Bidders coming to an auction for the first time should sit near the front, both to see the auctioneer clearly and to catch his attention easily if they wish to bid. Ideally, this should be done with a word plus an unmistakable gesture of the arm! Regular bidders sometimes want to pre-arrange a system of signals with the auctioneer because they do not wish to be seen to be bidding, but it is at the auctioneer's risk if he complies with such a request. In the event of legal action being brought where an auctioneer has agreed to a certain mode of bidding, such as keeping one's legs crossed or holding a pencil up vertically, and this has gone wrong owing to a misunderstanding as to whether the purchaser was continuing to bid or not, the courts are unlikely to

◆ AUCTION PREPARATION ◆

protect the auctioneer because there is so much room for misinterpretation. In a notorious instance at a leading art auction house, an arrangement was made whereby if a certain dealer was sitting down, he was bidding, if he bid openly he was bidding, if he stood up he had stopped bidding, and if he sat down again he was not bidding until he raised his finger. Having raised his finger he was bidding until he stood up. What hope had an auctioneer of following such a sequence correctly?

Identifying the Successful Bidder

As implied by the foregoing, it is vital for the auctioneer to identify the bidder clearly and correctly to the room. Firstly, it tells the bidder that his bid and no one else's has been accepted. Thus, when two bidders are sitting next to each other the auctioneer must find some way of distinguishing between them, picking out a green hat, blue tie, a red scarf or something not too tactless. He can, of course, call the bidder by name, or, more discreetly, by initial, if he knows it, though some people prefer a high degree of anonymity – hence the desire for secret signs – in the auction room.

Secondly, it indicates to the runners who need to know precisely and quickly, in a room of up to five hundred people, who is the successful bidder. Nowadays, however, most auctions are recorded on audio tape, and the opportunity to listen to the proceedings and identify the bidder can be essential, especially when someone tries to deny having bid. The recording of auctions can also pinpoint instances where the vendor bids the reserve price or above. Auctioneers generally provide for this eventuality in their terms with their clients, making the vendor liable for, say, double the commission (see p. 19 above, and for further discussion of this question, see chapter 9).

Controlling the Level of Bidding

Some auctioneers, as a matter of routine, are known to say that if the bidding is going in £10,000's they will not accept bids of say £500, even though they are above the reserve price. Whilst, according to the National Conditions of Sale, it is a matter for the auctioneer's discretion, it may, as a point of psychology, sometimes be better to allow the bidding to increase step by step. In the writer's experience, it once took sixty-nine bids to increase the price by £30,000, the winning bidder adding never more (or less) than £50 to the underbidder's bid. On that occasion, the purchaser had come to the auction on the spur of the moment – and he outbid a major building society.

Disclosed Reserves

Occasionally, in the case of an unusual and difficult to value property, the auctioneer may recommend disclosing the level of the reserve in the catalogue, in order to attract buyers. A ceiling figure is therefore given: 'reserve below £50,000', the actual reserve remaining a closely guarded secret.

Last Minute Changes of Reserves

A vendor may always change his reserve to a lower figure, even when the auctioneer has reached the rostrum. Auctioneers are not, however, always keen to raise the reserve price at the last minute; at least one firm states in the conditions that the reserve, once settled with the vendor, can only be increased with the auctioneer's consent.

Sealed Reserves

Auctioneers generally require in their terms with clients that reserves must be communicated to them at least two working days before the auction. In certain circumstances, however, clients may insist on sealed reserves. For instance, once the Charity Commissioners have approved the reserve, they transmit it to the auctioneer in a sealed envelope not to be opened until he is on the rostrum, in order to ensure complete confidentiality. Where there is some kind of dispute, between partners who are breaking up a partnership, say, or members of a family who are beneficiaries, the reserve may be kept under seal so that no one is unfairly favoured.

♦ AUCTION PREPARATION ♦

Occasionally, an auctioneer may receive a reserve in an envelope, on the morning of the sale in question, with specific instructions that it should only be opened on the rostrum when the lot is being offered. It is risky for him to respect such instructions to the letter as it might expose him to public embarrassment as when an auctioneer found that through a mistake there was just a blank piece of paper in the envelope: he had no alternative but to apologise and withdraw the property from the auction.

Withdrawn Bids

The purchaser has the right to withdraw his bid until the hammer has fallen. It is always the auctioneer's fear that he will do so if there is any lingering at the end. In the event of the under-bidder then declining to purchase at the figure he last bid, the auctioneer has little choice but to re-offer the lot to the room

Bidding on Behalf of Purchasers

Auctioneers are sometimes embarrassed by a request to make a bid on behalf of a purchaser, who cannot attend the sale, before a reserve has been fixed, thereby putting the auctioneer under a moral obligation to tell the vendor the figure that has been bid. Where the reserve is known, the auctioneer should ask the vendor whether he can bid for a purchaser, but without disclosing the amount involved.

Uncomfortable situations can still arise, for example, where a postal bid is twice the reserve price, particularly if it is the only bid, or where there is a last minute addendum and the auctioneer does not know whether the purchaser would still wish to bid in the new circumstances.

Should the RICS lay down professional guide-lines for real estate auctioneers, it might be fairer if written bids on behalf of purchasers were prohibited altogether. Similarly, telephone bidding, although successfully used at chattel auctions, could open the way to misunderstandings, if for example, messages were wrongly transmitted or addenda had not been brought to the attention of the absentee bidder.

◆ PROPERTY AUCTIONS ◆

Dutch Auctions

This is the method of descending bids and selling to the first bidder – the phrase is incorrectly used to refer to people being gazumped. These auctions are used, as the name suggests, in Holland, but very rarely in the United Kingdom. The writer once resorted to a Dutch auction when the successful bidder for a block of ground rents came up to the rostrum and said he had purchased the wrong lot. It was re-offered at the price at which it had been knocked down as the starting figure. The first bid was fortunately not very much lower.

◆

In conclusion, I should like to compare the auctioneer to the batsman who has to face a variety of medium and slow bowlers on different types of wickets. The questions like the cricket ball may come at any speed and pop up from any direction. The bowler has ten fielders to help him whereas the batsman is on his own and so is the auctioneer. He must protect his client just as the batsman protects his wicket. If he gives the wrong answer, it is like playing the wrong stroke and he is out!

· 3 ·

Individual Residential Properties

Peter Kearon FRICS, of Knight Frank & Rutley

'Residential' in the context of this chapter refers to property with vacant possession – usually an owner-occupied house or estate – sold individually at auction, a very different market in practice from the sale of residential investments (see chapter 4).

Before going into what is involved in selling such property under the hammer, it is appropriate to remind the reader that, irrespective of the advantages and disadvantages of the auction business, the agent or auctioneer should never lose sight of his basic responsibility, which is to achieve a sale to the client's best advantage, usually measured in terms of what can finally be banked.

Nine out of ten residential sales where there is vacant possession are sold by private treaty. The traumas of the usual sale negotiations are well known. Gazumping, or going to best offers by sealed bids, are commonplace practices in a strong or rising market. It is argued by some that a private treaty sale, handled with expertise, should achieve the best results. But the risk of losing the good buyer, having found him in the first place, is much reduced by selling through tender or auction, the latter usually public, but occasionally private, as explained below.

Tender documents, if properly drawn, can be made legally binding when a bid for the property is made. Although most sales are conducted by public or open tender, a limited or private tender, meaning that the documents are only made available to a pre-selected number of potential buyers, is equally effective when the circumstances are right, such as when the agent knows that the buyers for a particular development can be counted on the fingers of one hand and a public or open tender would achieve no more. The few pre-selected potential purchasers will invariably stretch themselves if they know that they are being offered a property on this basis.

Another approach is to put a property up for sale by private treaty or by auction later. This is a 'mixed dish', in effect a private treaty sale technique with an auction timetable, often notional, threatening the buyer. Usually, the vendor's aim is to avoid being tied down on price; it is a tactic favoured in a strong market by some well-heeled, hard-nosed London agents.

The Advantages and Disadvantages of a Sale by Auction

It is worth stating the elementary pros and cons which should affect the decision by the vendor or his agent as to whether to auction a particular residential property.

To start with the advantages: the immediate contract is probably the most important. The fall of the hammer constitutes a binding contract which is then formalised by a signature on the memorandum of sale which forms part of the printed sale particulars. A sharp bang does away with all the delays that are normally part of buying and selling houses. If the bidding fails to reach the reserve, it is very often possible to get agreement on price plus a signed contract immediately after the sale, before the excitement is lost and the buyers have left the room. Few vendors – and, more to the point, few genuine buyers – will resist the chance of tying up a sale in this way.

The sale is seen to be conducted in the public gaze. There can be no better way of satisfying the world in general that a particular property has been properly promoted and sold at the best price. This is an all important factor in dealing with the requirements of the traditional fiduciary client, i.e.

♦ INDIVIDUAL RESIDENTIAL PROPERTIES ♦

trustees, executors, mortgagees, liquidators and the like. Charities and public bodies can be confident that they have done their duty. Warring beneficiaries should be equally content that they are getting their fair share. A further advantage is that the vendor cannot be embarrassed by approaches after the sale. The house was known to be in the market so it was open to all to bid. This sort of situation is particularly relevant when the vendor has trustee status.

An auction provides a definite date to work to for both the actual sale and the completion date. A fixed timetable of this sort is often essential for a vendor facing expensive bridging finance in buying another house, while a known date and place for the sale concentrates the competition for the property.

Another advantage is the wide exposure to the market that an auction property inevitably receives. In the top firms, catalogues will be distributed to an extensive mailing list of buyers built up over a number of years as well as to adjoining occupiers, and to local agents, solicitors, banks and accountants (for typical particulars and Special Conditions of Sale, see Appendix 4). Furthermore, the auction will be advertised both nationally and locally and usually by a board erected on the property.

This comprehensive marketing means that the 'special purchaser' who, for whatever reason, is able to pay a price above that of the average buyer, is more readily located and persuaded to come to the room; also, of course, the extent of the marketing makes a sale by auction more accessible to the potential buyer who, in the case of a private treaty sale, might never have known that the property was available.

Particularly in the residential field, there are certain sorts of property where, because of their special nature, no one, be it the owner or the agent, can really be certain of the value. 'Unique' as a word is debased currency these days but from time to time such a place comes up for sale. How better to establish the correct market value than to take it to auction? The same principle applies to the existence of the 'special purchaser' where strong competition is already there.

In these happy circumstances, no prior commitment on price is put on the agent or his client. With luck and skilful marketing plus the human element of competition among buyers, the end price may stagger everyone. It follows that two bidders (not including the auctioneer) are needed to achieve that happy state.

In the residential field, the majority of buyers prefer to bid at auction rather than bidding blind – in other words, making a binding offer by tender: the opposition can be seen in the auction room; one bid more than the next man or woman is all that is needed to secure the property.

The catalogue of disadvantages of a sale by auction is well documented. The main ones are summarised here. Foremost, is the fact that the costs of sale for an owner-occupied house can be substantially higher than when selling by private treaty, as they generally have to cover the printing of high quality, illustrated auction particulars and an advertising budget tailored to the individual property. The enlightened vendor will realise, however, that these promotion expenses can easily be recovered by one bid in the room.

A sale by auction has, of necessity, an inflexible timetable, and the sale itself takes longer to mount than a private treaty exercise, where, conditions permitting, terms can sometimes be agreed, with a quick exchange of contracts to follow, within a few days of the property being put on to the market. An auction will usually need a ten to twelve week countdown from the date of receiving instructions from the client to go ahead (see chapter 2).

There is no choice as to whom the property is sold. Sometimes this is an all-important factor in residential property. A sale by private treaty or by tender allows the vendor to choose his buyer if he wants to.

The result of the sale becomes public knowledge, with the price reported in the press.

The terms of the sale are rigid and are set out in the Conditions of Sale. Neither party is in a position to discuss the terms on which the house is sold, for example, what is included in the sale or the timing of the completion date. As

♦ INDIVIDUAL RESIDENTIAL PROPERTIES ♦

a result, a sale by auction of a particular house may well discourage, for instance, the potential purchaser who has almost but not quite sold his own house and who is therefore unwilling to face the commitment of signing an auction contract on a certain day and landing himself with two houses.

The last and most important disadvantage of the auction method should never be forgotten by vendors or their agents. A failed auction invariably discredits the property, makes it stale and usually devalues it. Hence the importance of judging the reserve correctly and hence also the need for the vendor to take his agent's advice.

Vendors

The residential agent and auctioneer will have very different vendors from those who make up the regular clientele in the commercial field. Each will have his own idea of how much the auctioneer should be doing for him, since in this market the client is primarily the owner-occupier who is selling his house. The more expensive the house, the more sophisticated and demanding he may be; a sympathetic ear, considerable patience and a good bedside manner are essential attributes in the business. Clients disposing of a valuable London or country house or estate require time and trouble to be spent on their property. They are not to be compared with the speculator or developer off-loading ten or twenty lots which form part of a two-day sale.

Each private client will want at least one meeting to discuss sale by auction; meetings with the client's solicitor will usually be necessary to finalise the instructions and progress the legal work. Further meetings, leading up to fixing the reserve, will often be called for. The same standard of individual attention will be expected of the auctioneer and his firm by the professional client who is behind the instructions to mount an executor, mortgagee or liquidator's sale.

The bigger the firm of agents and the higher their reputation, the greater the expectations of the client. For example, it is often taken for granted, particularly in the London

♦ PROPERTY AUCTIONS ♦

area, that people wanting to look at the house should be accompanied by the agent. This can mean numerous visits at untoward times. The prudent agent provides for some realistic expenses in agreeing the costs of the sale at the outset. Woe betide him if this is not done. In short, the vendor's expectations, at the top end of the residential market, go far beyond the long established text-book legal duties of the auctioneer towards his client, and call for loyalty, care and obedience!

When to Sell Residential Property at Auction

We come now to the all important question – in what sort of circumstances is a residential property with vacant possession best sold at auction? Some examples from a range of such properties auctioned will highlight the general principles involved.

We have already noted that the trustee or similar client's property is the ideal auction subject. A good example of this was the sale of a small but obviously valuable freehold house in Mayfair, one of several assets of a Middle Eastern businessman who had gone bankrupt worldwide for a very large sum; a well-known firm of accountants was left to pick up the pieces. The price the house fetched (£1.3 million) barely covered a handful of the debts. On the other hand, if the property had not been taken to public auction, the receiver would still be dealing with the claims from unhappy creditors who would all know someone who would have paid much more for the place.

Another instance of acting for executors was the sale of a house in Highgate owned and lived in for some forty years by the senior partner of a firm of solicitors who died intestate, his affairs in a muddle, the house in a mess and the family at loggerheads: none of the beneficiaries could agree what the house was worth. It was sold at auction in 1982 for a six-figure sum, which was considered to be very high in those days, after more than a hundred prospective buyers had been shown round. The family were obliged to agree its value.

♦ INDIVIDUAL RESIDENTIAL PROPERTIES ♦

Earlier, reference was made to the sort of property where, because of its special nature, no one can be certain of its value. The following were exceptional properties put to auction: a somewhat rundown listed Regency villa in its own third of an acre garden, in Regent's Park, London, offered for sale on a new sixty-year lease with the buyer committed to spending a large sum on modernisation – a rare house and very difficult to value. It sold to a man who had seen it in the dark on a rainy night the day before the sale. Similarly, a very pretty, early Georgian house in a fashionable London suburb, with a big garden so that it was more like a country house, was justifiably describable as 'unique' and therefore hard to price. In the event, after nearly two hundred people had been over it, several pre-auction offers received and rejected by the executors on advice, it was knocked down in a crowded room to one of half a dozen buyers for nearly half a million pounds (in 1982): again, an example of what can be achieved with strong competition for a special house.

Turning to the country, it was anyone's guess what a three-bedroom stone-built cottage, in a lovely position overlooking a rocky cove on the Dorset coast, would fetch, and the sale aroused great local interest. From a reserve of £30,000, two builders took it up, with intervals for 'refreshment', to £64,000, a lot of money in 1973.

Another good candidate for a sale under the hammer is the unimproved property, be it in London or outside; it will attract the private purchaser who has ideas of how he or she can renovate the place at minimal cost and with maximum benefit to the value, and who is happy to compete with the professionals in this specialised field. The end result is invariably in excess of expectations.

A further example of a residential property best sold at auction is where something obviously valuable and saleable is hedged with complications of the sort that would give any buyer's lawyer a field day: for instance, a short lease on two large adjoining buildings in Belgravia, ideal for conversion into expensive flats, but with no terms quoted for an extension of the lease by the freeholders and a threatened

♦ PROPERTY AUCTIONS ♦

preservation order on two of the rooms where Chopin was known to have played during a visit to London in 1848. In these sorts of circumstances, the private treaty buyer can string out negotiations indefinitely. Faced with an auction timetable and the immediate contract, a handful of property developers were happy to bid furiously against each other.

From the foregoing, it can be seen that given the standard requirement of trustees or similar fiduciary client, their property is best sold at auction. It can also be argued that, assuming a good market, the auction method is correct for either the very best or prime property, or the unimproved property with obvious potential. At the bottom end of the scale, there is traditionally the poorest type of property where wide publicity and a quick death at a down-to-earth reserve is the best way to dispose of it.

Private Auctions

Turning to the role of the private auction, it is, in essence, the best way of resolving a situation where private treaty negotiations get out of hand and circumstances rule out resolving the unpleasantness by calling for best offers or sealed bids. A necessary condition, however, of a successful private auction is strong competition from the buyers. Each is invited to attend the agent's office at a specified time, having been warned that the rules of auction will apply, namely that there will be a contract at the fall of the hammer and that the vendor's solicitor, armed with a contract, will be in attendance in the room. More important, there is a disclosed reserve – usually the original guide price or private treaty asking price and the buyer's attendance at the sale signifies a willingness to enter into an immediate contract at that figure or better. In short, it is an auction by invitation only.

A good example of this method being used was the sale in the early 1980s of an old-fashioned, but potentially very appealing freehold house, in Chelsea. The guide price was nearly half a million. A handful of buyers with long pockets were all prepared to gazump each other indefinitely. With a

♦ INDIVIDUAL RESIDENTIAL PROPERTIES ♦

private auction the house was sold in less than ten minutes to a television personality who outbid the field and added £150,000 to the price. It is worth noting that a sale by auction had originally been recommended, this advice being unacceptable to the client because of the length of time necessary to prepare a sale. In the event, one month later a private auction achieved a price that was a record at the time, and none of the buyers could complain that they were not given a fair chance.

Another successful private auction was the sale in the 1970s of a short lease of a Mayfair house being keenly fought over by a number of foreign buyers. The vendor had evidently pledged to sell to several of them and shaken them each individually by the hand. In the circumstances, the buyers became wary of pursuing negotiations any further but, faced with a private auction, they bid well above the disclosed reserve, the successful bidder being a runner for a Middle Eastern prince with an open cheque book and orders to buy at any price!

Pre-Auction Sales

Finally, we come to the contentious subject of when and if it is right to sell before auction. In the writer's experience, pre-emptive bids aimed at securing the property are invariably repeated and improved upon in the auction room, despite statements made at the time of such a bid that it is now or never.

In the early 1970s when London house prices were moving up at an unprecedented rate (it may be noted that gazumping was an unknown way of life at that time), it was often the practice to go to auction for almost any worthwhile house. Although the results of these sales may seem small beer thanks to subsequent inflation, at the time the prices achieved were invariably an education to the buyer and often to the agent as well. Certainly all pre-auction bids, of which there were many, were well exceeded in the saleroom. The situation has not changed since. On the other hand, on the rare occasion when only one buyer can be seen on the horizon

♦ PROPERTY AUCTIONS ♦

and he is keen to sign a pre-auction contract on the printed particulars at a figure that will satisfy the client, it must be in his interest to agree the purchase and cancel the auction. The auctioneer, on the other hand, will not be willing to do this too often or his reputation will suffer. Buyers generally like to rely on having a fair chance to bid for their chosen house, particularly if they have been encouraged to go to the expense both of instructing their solicitors to carry out searches and of having the house surveyed, and have taken time off to attend the auction.

It is evident from this chapter that a fundamental characteristic of auction practice in the residential field is that each sale depends on special treatment, culminating in a polite eulogy from the rostrum lasting twenty minutes or so, with, as likely as not, the vendor glowering at the auctioneer from the back of the room and defying him to fail to mention some salient feature of the property. Not all vendors turn up on the day: at least one has been known to go to church instead.

These individual performances are a far cry from the crowded gatherings in the Grosvenor House Hotel or the Connaught Rooms with some five hundred dealers leafing through a thick catalogue and with each lot taking no more than a couple of minutes of the auctioneer's time to knock down before he is on to the next. What should be common ground, to both activities, however, is an unrivalled working knowledge of the market-place. How otherwise can the auctioneer advise his clients on the proper reserve? It will also be appreciated that auctions of residential property, as described in this chapter, do not take place all that often, thus the auctioneer will only find the right material if his firm maintains a sizeable register of saleable houses.

Each sale has its own sense of occasion and needs to be seen as a small but valued part of the overall picture, which, in essence, is disposing of the client's property to the best advantage.

• 4 •

Residential Investment

Clifford G. Murphy FRICS

Supply and Demand

Few properties are unsuitable for auction, only those which will fail to engender competitive bidding. In the case of residential investments there is a constant demand and, since it is always greater than the supply, it produces the ideal conditions for an auction.

The appeal of residential investment to investors, both large and small, has been strengthened by the effects of rent control and security of tenure which have increased the reversionary value and the difference between investment value and vacant possession value. It is this situation rather than yield – generally between one and ten per cent – that creates the demand. Successive legislation has made the ultimate reversion to vacant possession more important, thereby further encouraging, along with inflation, such investment.

Supply has been affected by several contradictory factors. On the one hand, the continuance of rent control and security of tenure have caused the number of residential investment properties to diminish, as ultimate reversions to vacant possession usually lead to the sale of the building (although initiatives to encourage the private rented sector are constantly on the horizon). Diminution in the supply has also been brought about by sitting tenants in both the private and the public sector purchasing their property, and by the lack of new building and letting.

On the other hand, both industry and parts of the public sector have needed to divest themselves of residential holdings. In the past, industry and the public utilities provided housing for their workforces in order to attract labour, but, with inflation taking hold of the property market, employees have realised that to become a 'tenant at will' in rented accommodation has prevented their enjoying the capital appreciation and inflation from which owner-occupiers benefit. No longer does the offer of accommodation with a job carry the same weight.

Thus, bodies like the Metropolitan Police, the British Rail Property Board, the Health Authorities and many other concerns, public and private, have been selling off their residential property – usually by auction in order not only to achieve a successful sale but also to be seen publicly to be disposing of the property at the best price available.

Clearly, this is an area of the property market where there is a certain amount of luck and speculation. For instance, on one occasion a regular buyer purchased a tenanted house only to discover he had bought the wrong lot. On visiting his mistaken purchase, he was astonished and delighted to discover the sitting tenant in the process of moving out.

It is not of course advisable for prospective investors to rely entirely upon chance. The buyer who does his homework and bids accordingly will ultimately come off best. Unfortunately, in a market dominated by regular purchasers, a diligent buyer often becomes known as such and is then outbid by speculators who may not even have seen the property but who are attracted to it because he is bidding.

The Auction Catalogue and Auction Location

Unlike the residential field described in the previous chapter, residential investments are best sold through a comprehensive auction catalogue with as many lots as can be handled with adequate time and attention in one auction session. With such a catalogue, well-advertised, the auctioneers can

◆ RESIDENTIAL INVESTMENT ◆

rely upon a good attendance and invest in a large auction room. Likewise, a healthy number of catalogues can be printed and distributed to a wide variety of buyers. This will benefit the less saleable lots by exposing them to a well-packed auction room, and its consequent advantages.

Whereas certain types of property are best sold on their home ground by an auctioneer with local knowledge and experience, residential investments tend to be brought to the market-place in London. Public bodies, such as the British Rail Property Board or the National Coal Board, find it more convenient when dealing with a scattered portfolio to sell through the medium of a central auction which will command the attention of investors nationally; they will still attempt to capture local interest by appropriate advertising.

Searches and Pre-Auction Preparation

As with normal preparations for an auction (see chapters 1 and 2, above), residential investments require careful local searches. Such a search might uncover in this context:

A Closing Order A closing order under the Housing Acts forbids human occupation of a dwelling in its present condition. A property cannot be advertised as a dwelling house, or a room as a living room, if a closing order exists to forbid its use as such.

Outstanding Notices – under the Housing or Public Health Acts It is not enough to rely on the standard clause in the Conditions of Sale stating that the purchaser is assumed to have made his own searches (see p. 44 below), such notices should be disclosed, and the liability for compliance as between vendor and purchaser should be settled prior to auction. It is to the advantage of the vendor to agree this matter beforehand to avoid a situation where the auctioneer is unable adequately to answer questions from the floor and the consequent uncertainty compromises the sale.

Listed Buildings or Tree Preservation Orders Such matters could be a selling point; equally, a failure to disclose such information could be regarded as misrepresentation if there was an implication that the property had potential redevelopment value.

Notice Pursuant to Section 19 of the Housing Act 1961 In the case of *Topfell Ltd v Galley Properties Ltd* (1978) 249 EG 341, a house was offered with part vacant possession. The first floor was let and the ground floor vacant. The property was sold only for it to be discovered that Croydon Borough Council had issued a direction under section 19 restricting the occupation of the property to one family only. The High Court upheld the purchaser's contention that the description of the ground floor as 'vacant' implied that this floor could be occupied. It should be noted that the inclusion in the Conditions of Sale in the contract in question, of the standard clause referred to above where it states that the purchaser is assumed to have made his own searches and pre-contract enquiries, was not considered to put all the responsibility on to the buyer – *caveat emptor* ('let the buyer beware') – and the Court ordered the purchase price to be reduced.

It is worth noting that in a recent case, *Rignall Developments v Halil* [1987] 1EGLR 193, the Court again took the view that, although the purchaser had failed to make pre-contract searches, the vendor was not protected by that clause in the Conditions of Sale, from failing to indicate that there was a registered local land charge relating to a housing improvement grant of which the landlord had availed himself under the 1974 Housing Act (and which he would be required to repay if he sold the property within five years of receiving it). The Court found in favour of the purchaser on the grounds that the vendor had failed to show good title. At the same time, it regretted the delays by local authorities, particularly in London, in handling local searches and the resultant inability of prospective purchasers to obtain them before auctions took place.

The Landlord and Tenant Act 1987 With the introduction of this Act, which gives long leasehold tenants, in particular,

◆ RESIDENTIAL INVESTMENT ◆

in blocks of flats, new rights (a block of flats being any premises containing more than two flats), the auctioneer needs to ascertain that where more than fifty per cent of the tenants are qualifying tenants (i.e. not under a protected shorthold or business tenancy), they have been given the first refusal on disposal. Only if they do not serve an acceptance notice within the period specified in the landlord's notice (minimum two months), is the landlord free to dispose as he thinks fit (subject to certain conditions). In the event of a landlord failing to serve a notice before selling, the succeeding landlord could find himself having to dispose of his interest to the tenants by way of a purchase notice. In addition, it may be noted that under the Act the idle landlord who fails to maintain his property could in certain circumstances have his interest compulsorily purchased by qualifying tenants; this also has implications for succeeding landlords howsoever they have purchased the property.

On the Rostrum

The auctioneer needs a realistic reserve price in order to put the property on the market at an appropriate point of the bidding. An announcement that the reserve has been passed will invariably stimulate the bidding, though it should not be made immediately but rather when interest starts to flag. The audience should not know that the auctioneer is struggling to reach the reserve, and he should only let them know that it has been passed when it suits him.

The professional bidder is a facet of residential investment auctions. He usually keeps a very low profile, waiting for his property to be put in the market and for the bidding to reach its conclusion before he comes into the picture. This is where the auctioneer with long experience of his market and of his buyers is able to get the feel of the room and know when and where he can extract the bids.

There are several ways the auctioneer can resuscitate the bidding if necessary. Take, for instance, a residential investment described in the catalogue as being let on a regulated tenancy. The tenant, Mrs Black, is eighty-six years old and

♦ PROPERTY AUCTIONS ♦

has no relatives living with her who could claim a tenancy by succession. That information is best kept up the auctioneer's sleeve. Meanwhile, the reserve is £12,000 and the bidding has stopped short of £11,500. Before attempting to plead for further bids, the auctioneer might carry on as follows: 'Oh, by the way, when you inspected the property did you meet our tenant, Mrs Black? Charming old lady isn't she? She tells me she is over eighty-six . . . Sorry sir, what was your bid? £11,750, £12,000, £12,250, thank you' – a pause in the bidding – 'I feel rather sorry for Mrs Black – she is living in this house completely on her own with no apparent relatives living with her to take over the tenancy . . . Yes I'll take another £100 Sir, £12,350, £12,450, £12,550 . . . Yes the property is in the market, thank you another £100, £200, £300.' If the auctioneer handles the situation correctly, then not only will he introduce a touch of humour and so relax the room, but he will be using his expertise and experience to extract the last possible bid and the highest possible price for his client.

While the audience knows what is happening, they also know that such statements are not made frivolously as they could be construed as a warranty. The dividing line between a puff and a warranty is very fine. 'This well-maintained house' is probably just the former, but 'this structurally sound house' is most certainly the latter (for more on warranties, see chapter 9).

More difficult is the approach to unfavourable information, for example, when a dwelling is subject to an improvement notice. Having described the property, the auctioneer might go on to say, 'Have you all made your searches on this property? Go on, ask me if I have a search! Thank you Mr Brown, for asking me that question; yes indeed, we do have a search. It reveals that the property is in a General Improvement Area, and we do in fact have an improvement notice. What a fortunate situation, the property does not have a bathroom, but you will be able to make such improvements and obtain a discretionary improvement grant for such improvements.' This demonstrates the value of having made the searches and been in possession of all possible information at an early date, to enable the auctioneer not only to disclose such facts, to avoid an abortive contract, but to present them to advantage. Anyone can sell the property which is in such demand that it is difficult even to record the bids quickly enough, but the successful auctioneer has to be able to cope with almost any proposition that he may be called upon to handle.

The possibility of statutory notices and other hidden drawbacks to residential investment property can encourage people to ask potentially embarrassing questions in order to dampen the bidding. For example: 'Mr Auctioneer, can you please tell us something about the outstanding Public Health notice?' A suitable answer would be: 'Yes Mr K. I'm glad you asked that question, I believe you have already had a copy of the notice and have been informed by my staff that it is the vendor's intention to comply with it himself. I believe, apart from sash cords, the only other item that the sanitary inspector could find to put on his notices was a bit of plaster work in the kitchen. Now, Mr K., I am pleased to see that you are interested in this desirable property, and I can fully understand your attempts to dampen any opposition. Perhaps you would like to start the bidding.' A bidder of this sort may start off with a very low bid which will be dismissed out of hand. He obviously wants the property, and when he does come into the bidding seriously, the auctioneer might say, 'Ah, Mr K., I thought you were worried about the sash cords.' All this is done with good humour, the auctioneer never getting ruffled, but attempting to turn everything to his advantage and to create an atmosphere of good humour, for the whole audience to enjoy.

The last thing an auctioneer wants is to face a sea of vacant faces ready to depress the market. The auctioneer should not bore his audience by repeating everything in the catalogue: all that is necessary is to highlight certain salient points, and here again the extra bits of verbal information, which he may be able to produce, will attract attention and enliven the proceedings.

♦ PROPERTY AUCTIONS ♦

Upon concluding the auction, the auctioneer should make sure that all successful purchasers sign their memoranda and pay their deposits before leaving the room, and he should make a statement to that effect. It is essential to remember that for the period when the auctioneer is on the rostrum, he is deemed by law to be acting for both vendor and purchaser, and in that capacity he is able to sign both parts of the contract, if the purchaser fails to do so. It is therefore important that the auctioneer remains on the rostrum until such time as all contracts have been signed. Once he has left the room, he is then only acting for the vendor and has lost his right to sign for the purchaser.

Auction Results

Finally, it is worth adding a note on analysing auction results for residential investments. It must be emphasised that the calculation of what a property realises at a sale is based upon a percentage of the vacant possession value and not yield. Investment value is based upon (1) the age of the tenant (2) the ultimate vacant possession value in view of inflation (3) the existence or not of sub-tenants and (4) the existence or not of next of kin who live in the property and who could inherit the tenancy by right of transmission. It may be considered indiscreet or tasteless for an auctioneer to list such facts in his catalogue, and he would need to be very certain of his information to do so, but these are relevant factors which affect the value of a residential investment in the auction room. In popular suburbs of London, residential investments where the above factors are favourable to the potential buyer have produced about sixty-five to seventy per cent of vacant possession value at auction. If these properties were offered at such prices by private treaty, there is little doubt that they would be rejected as over-priced.

· 5 ·

Residential Land

Christopher Drury FRICS, *of Jones Lang Wootton*

The popularity of auctions has focused on the success of selling secondary retail and residential property. Without quite the same publicity the sale of land for residential development by auction has enjoyed similar success for a number of years. Arguably, such property constitutes the most challenging and, hence, the most rewarding auction material: it is not the easiest commodity to value and it demands special attention to timing (in marketing terms), quality and availability of information and brochure presentation. On the day of the sale itself, it is more likely than any other type of property to provoke awkward questions or disruption by local action groups or residents' associations.

Despite this, many vendors prefer to market sites in this way in order to clinch a definite contract and avoid the mire of options, conditional contracts, protracted negotiations, extended loans or contracts which are always going to be exchanged tomorrow. Purchasers are frequently battle hardened after years of the cut and thrust of site-finding, and are undaunted by the prospect of investing time in making pre-auction enquiries and bidding on the day. Residential sites, therefore, are well suited to sale by auction.

◆ PROPERTY AUCTIONS ◆

Obtaining Preliminary Information

In taking instructions to sell residential land, it is essential to obtain at the outset fundamental information relating to the site and its development including:

1. precise extent of site;
2. planning documents as appropriate e.g. application forms and accompanying plans, planning consents (detailed or outline), development briefs, appeal documents;
3. section 52 agreements (see below, p. 53);
4. proximity of available services;
5. tenancies, agreements, licences, easements, wayleaves;
6. clarification of access arrangements;
7. soil and (where appropriate) level surveys;
8. known development problems, both physical and environmental;
9. restrictive covenants;
10. tree preservation orders;
11. a general history of the site.

In certain cases, it might be appropriate to organise surveys to monitor the effect of noise or vibration from nearby undertakings. Without such information it will be difficult to provide even a preliminary opinion of value, which is fundamental to advising the vendor as to an appropriate reserve.

The Brochure

The style of presentation is the prerogative of the auctioneer, but certain information is essential to encourage interest and answer basic questions.

Photographs It is frequently said that one photograph is worth a thousand words and this is true of residential sites. In this context particular consideration should be given to using an aerial photograph even if the cost is relatively high (£150-200 at 1987 prices); a special advantage of such photo-

◆ RESIDENTIAL LAND ◆

graphs is that it will show not only the site concerned but also the surroundings, which may provide an attractive setting, and indicate adjacent and complementary occupants.

Certain firms that specialise in such photography also maintain a library and it may be possible to acquire a shot of the site 'off the shelf', particularly if it is located in a major urban area. It is of course important to indicate on the photograph as accurately as possible the extent of the site.

A word of warning: weather or flying restrictions can cause considerable delays and, therefore, it is imperative to make arrangements at a very early stage for an aerial photograph to be taken. The photographer needs careful briefing so that he knows exactly which is the site in question.

The Plan This is arguably the single most important item in the brochure. Not only must it show the precise area to be sold, but it can also be used to indicate wayleaves (sewers, cables, water courses, etc.) and easements (including rights of way) and the extent of tenancies; reference to the plan may be contained in the Special Conditions of Sale to delineate the reservations or liabilities to be imposed on the purchaser, for example, fencing.

Proofs of the plan to be used in the brochure must be carefully vetted by both the vendor and the solicitor to check the accuracy of the boundaries against the title deeds and to ensure that the colouring or other marking tallies with the references in the Special Conditions of Sale. Further, a matter which can frequently be overlooked: the plan should be checked against those used in connection with the planning application to ensure that they conform. It may be, for example, that the application and subsequent consent relate to a more extensive area than that being offered for sale.

The Text The text should be restricted to the provision of factual information including the following:

1. Location, description of the general area and the site's location, both geographical and in relation to the town centre, local shops, schools, public transport. Population

figures might also be included. The location may well be a major factor influencing the suitability of a site for sheltered housing which is generally more valuable than conventional residential development.
2. Description: the site, its features and boundaries, the site area, any buildings or other structures, reference to easements, wayleaves, etc.
3. Tenure: freehold or leasehold including terms of the lease.
4. Tenancies, licences, agreements: these are very important. Particular reference should be made to provisions for termination.
5. Planning: reference to the consent (if any) or development brief. This may be confined to a short description of the type of development for which consent has been granted. Where possible densities should be stated.
6. Local authorities.
7. Services available: gas, electricity, water, drains and sewers. Addresses and telephone numbers of appropriate authorities.
8. Schedule of documents available for inspection: planning documents (applications and consents); planning or development briefs; soil surveys; leases and agreements; other relevant plans and drawings; local searches.
9. Solicitors.

Planning

There are many traps for the unwary and a working knowledge of planning is important; no residential development site is ever totally straightforward. Set out below are typical problem areas but it should be appreciated that no such list can be exhaustive.

All planning permissions contain conditions: some are routine, others are more onerous. Each must be considered to ascertain whether it is possible for the development to comply. A check should be made in the local authority's register of applications to ensure that the consent document provided by the vendor is the only relevant one. Plans

◆ RESIDENTIAL LAND ◆

accompanying the application must be checked to see whether the permission relates to the exact area being sold; otherwise it might not be possible to implement the development without the need to resubmit an application relating to the subject site alone.

Occasionally, a consent requires the co-operation of one or more third parties: for example, suitable access to the land may be across another property, in which case formal agreement with the owners should have been negotiated prior to marketing. It may be that a previous or adjoining owner controls access on to the development site by retaining a strip of land between the site and the connecting road. The possible existence of these so-called 'blackmail' or 'ransom' strips (since they are used to extort substantial sums from the site owner/developer) should be investigated to avoid last minute hiccoughs. In similar vein, any section 52 agreements (made under that section of the 1971 Town and Country Planning Act, and allowing local authorities to regulate or restrict development by agreement with the landowner or developer, usually to their mutual benefit) should be capable of being complied with. It is also important to assess the financial implications of such an agreement which may affect the value of the site.

The conscientious auctioneer should be prepared to discuss with the vendor the implications of more onerous conditions and consider their effect on saleability and price. Occasionally planning conditions are imposed which might be deemed to be *ultra vires*, i.e. beyond the powers of the planning authority; in such cases it may be appropriate to obtain counsel's opinion. Removal of the effect of such conditions is likely to enhance the value of the land.

Frequently the provision of sight lines or vision splays are imposed as a condition of development. It is essential to ensure that such a condition is capable of being complied with; it may occasionally be necessary to come to some arrangement with adjoining owners.

The density of permitted development is always a matter for review. A permission granted a few years previously may be out of date as far as permitted density is concerned. The advent of sheltered housing schemes appears to have struck a responsive chord with planning authorities who may be prepared, particularly in more rural areas, to permit greater density. In cases where a site is being offered for sale subject to what might be deemed a low density (i.e. in a situation whereby it might reasonably be expected that a greater number of habitable rooms might be permitted) then a 'claw-back' clause might be considered for inclusion in the Special Conditions of Sale. Typically this would involve an extra payment per additional habitable room (according to a predetermined formula) being made by the purchaser to the vendor in the event of consent for a greater density being obtained (and implemented) within a specific time-scale. But the inclusion of a 'claw-back' clause does not necessarily have the desired effect: it may even depress the price unless there is enough incentive for the purchaser to go for a more intensive scheme.

To turn to development briefs, it is essential for the auctioneer to arrange a meeting with the local planning authority to discuss the implications of the brief. Although the brief will enshrine the principle of development on the site, the planning authorities should be consulted to ascertain their preferred type and density of development. Development briefs may require the purchaser to provide some community facility; the nature and extent of this should be fully discussed. If, for example, this is likely to be burdensome to a developer, the flexibility in attitude of the planners needs to be assessed.

Joint Sales

Occasionally two or more landowners agree to a joint sale. This may occur if a local authority wishes a number of adjoining sites to be developed comprehensively and issues a blanket consent. Alternatively, the development of one piece of land may be impossible, for, say, access reasons, without the co-operation of another owner. The details of

♦ RESIDENTIAL LAND ♦

the arrangement, e.g. the apportionment of the purchase price, are not relevant as far as this chapter is concerned but, nevertheless, a word of warning to the auctioneer and joint vendors is useful. Before marketing commences, there needs to be a binding agreement between parties to stop a quick-witted developer seeking to divide and conquer by buying up one ownership separately at a tempting price and then effectively thwarting an open-market selling campaign of the remainder by refusing to co-operate with other would-be purchasers. The other owners may find themselves forced to deal with just one party – never a situation conducive to obtaining the best price.

The Inspection

The amount of care required to be exercised during the inspection of a development site should not be under-estimated; particular attention should be paid to the following items:

Boundaries These need checking to see that they are clearly defined on site and tally with plans provided. It may be necessary to arrange for ill-defined boundaries to be pegged out clearly. Any apparent encroachments need to be clarified.

Potential Development Problems A professionally prepared soil survey is the best insurance but in its absence, tell-tale signs of waste or general dumping should be noted as they are likely to prompt questions from potential purchasers since, for instance, certain materials can create noxious chemical reactions as they corrode or decompose. Streams or marshy land in the vicinity may be indications that the land is prone to flooding and this should be checked. Mature trees should be noted in case preservation orders have been imposed.

Minerals A site which has been worked for minerals, e.g. gravel, may have been filled and the quality of that fill should be checked. If gravel extraction is prolific in the area there may be a special value attributable to the land prior to development. Again this should be investigated and featured in the brochure.

Easements Rights of way may not always be documented and could give rise to awkward questions on the day; the existence of well-worn paths should therefore be checked out. Other obvious intrusions may be telegraph poles or wires and electricity pylons or cables; less obvious may be water courses, gas or water mains or underground cables. The route of such items should if possible be shown on the plan contained in the brochure.

Access Existing points of access and potential for other access routes should be noted.

Acts of Occupation Any occupation of the site will usually be documented in leases, licences or agreements which indicate the degree of security of tenure and the ease with which possession may be obtained. But a cussed or determined occupier may take time to dislodge, however flimsy his rights to occupation; even illegal squatters (for example, gypsies) may only be evicted after a court order has been obtained. Quite unwittingly, the vendor may have allowed a tenancy situation to have been created conferring a degree of security of tenure: for instance, where there are cattle on the land – are they there under the provisions of a grazing agreement or an agricultural tenancy?

Marketing

Residential land demands patience. It is unwise to enter a site into an auction at the last moment since it may take time to gather together the many documents to be available for inspection (planning applications, consent documents, plans, soil surveys) and to identify problems such as are discussed above. Frequently the vendor is unaware of or has failed to recognise real difficulties.

Purchasers of residential land tend to launch a greater barrage of questions than for any other type of property and need to carry out a range of prior investigations, unlike bidders for, say, secondary commercial investments who frequently buy from the catalogue without even having seen the property concerned.

The timing of the marketing campaign is, therefore, crucial to success. Although there are no absolute rules, first advertisements should appear six or eight weeks before the day of the auction. This will allow bidders adequate time to make their enquiries particularly of the planning authority. Auction catalogues will be mailed as a matter of course to national and local house builders, estate agents active in the area or in residential development, housing associations, the relevant local authorities, adjoining owners and major landowners in the vicinity, as well as to those who respond to the advertising.

It is important to have prepared ready for immediate despatch to interested parties a package of additional information; typically this will include: copies of planning consent documents; accompanying plans; soil survey. As it is not always practical to send out all relevant information, a full set of documents must be available at both the vendor's solicitors and the auctioneer's offices. If considerable interest in the site is anticipated it is sensible to forewarn the local planning authority that the land is to be auctioned and that numerous planning enquiries should be expected.

The arrangements for access on to the land for inspection by potential bidders are important. Some sites are totally open and may present no problem; for others, it may be appropriate for the brochure to advise as to the arrangements for inspection. A problem with sites which provide easy access for inspection is that they also provide easy access for squatters whose presence may be totally disruptive and create a bad impression during the marketing period. Discussions should be held with the vendor to consider the best way to protect the site.

The Auction

Residential land may be auctioned locally or in London. In the latter case, it may either form part of a large commercial

◆ PROPERTY AUCTIONS ◆

sale, although offered in a separate catalogue, or be one of three or four residential land lots being sold off by a major landowner, such as British Rail, at one sale.

When a single piece of residential land is put to auction locally, it may well attract a room full of people only a few of whom are there to bid. For, the very nature of development sites can provide an emotive response from local residents who may well unite in opposition to any scheme. If some are motivated purely by self-interest ('no development at the bottom of my garden'), others may have sincerely-held views, for example, on conservation. Whatever the fundamental cause, a well-organised action group can provide a serious challenge which may culminate in disruption in the room on the day of the auction. This may take the form of a demonstration or, more likely, someone will seek to interrupt the proceedings to make a statement or to ask questions. Each auctioneer will have his own technique for dealing with the situation but he should try to anticipate it and, if possible, familiarise himself with the likely grounds of opposition. There might even be circumstances when it would be appropriate to deal with potentially belligerent demonstrations by arranging for the presence of security guards at the sale.

It would be wrong to end this chapter on an aggressive note. In the writer's experience development sites are the most consistently demanding type of auction lot, because of the amount of preparatory work involved. Furthermore, residential sites can prove difficult to value, making advice on reserves hard to give, particularly in an area where such sites are rarely marketed openly. But it is the demanding nature of the commodity which makes residential land the most exciting and rewarding of all auction property.

• 6 •

Commercial Property

Clive Carpenter FRICS, *of Allsop & Co*

As indicated elsewhere in this book, property auctions have come a long way in the last few years in both residential and commercial real estate, the two principal sectors of the property market. Those firms which spearheaded the auction boom in the early 1980s tended to concentrate on whichever of these two sectors had been their traditional area of practice.

It is interesting to note that the well-known commercial property auctioneers do not operate in isolation, but are supported by a well-established general practice with extensive investment, valuation, agency and professional expertise, while residential auctioneers have a full residential estate agency service. It was these support services departments which originally produced properties for sale and it is this historical background which explains the traditional demarcation between commercial and residential auctions. It is only very recently that the barriers have started to be broken down, as the auction side of some firms has outgrown and come to dominate the firm's original base and to accommodate both the commercial and residential disciplines.

To the outside observer the most obvious difference between the two sectors is the size of the lots offered. Less apparent is the additional expertise required of the commercial auctioneer, owing in part to the very nature and scope of commercial property and in part to the type of vendor

◆ PROPERTY AUCTIONS ◆

and purchaser involved. In all fields, the auctioneer's experience of the market and his constant link with prospective purchasers and ability to ascertain the level of interest in a particular lot are essential in advising the vendor on when and how to sell and at what price. When it comes to the auction itself, the commercial auctioneer, like the auctioneer of residential investments, will know his regular buyers, the manner in which they bid and the lots likely to be of interest to them. He will know who can be coaxed to bid an extra £1,000 and who cannot and he will know who needs to bid discreetly in order to avoid publicity or attracting the unwanted attention of rival bidders.

Commercial Properties Suitable for Auction

The types of commercial property that are considered suitable for auction, can be divided into two broad categories: those that will prove popular and will therefore generate competition in the auction room and realise a price in excess of expectations; and conversely those for which there is likely to be minimal demand and which therefore will benefit from the extensive marketing that only an auctioneer, with numerous lots in his catalogue, can employ.

The first category is, generally, by far the largest, and in the commercial field is currently dominated by good secondary shop investments, either single units or parades. While fashions change in property investment as in other markets and yields fluctuate accordingly, most commercial auctioneers would agree that an ideal auction lot in 1987 would be a small parade of shops with residential upper parts, whether located just off-pitch in a market town or forming the neighbourhood shopping outlet for a reasonably wealthy residential area. A typical yield range would be eight to ten per cent. Such a lot would appeal to many kinds of investor, from the private family trust looking for security with long-term growth, to the property dealer recognising break-up potential and, more recently, even to some more forward-thinking institutions.

The advantage of an auction is that the differing invest-

♦ COMMERCIAL PROPERTY ♦

ment objectives of the various potential purchasers will enable them to value on differing bases and the auction will have the effect of 'flushing out' the highest bidder in the room. A private treaty sale, with a fixed quoting price, cannot do this so well, as each potential buyer is working to reach the set figure, rather than trying to arrive at the maximum price he can afford to pay.

It necessarily follows from the foregoing, that any property which is likely to appeal to a 'special purchaser', who, for whatever reason, is usually able to pay more than its market value, is eminently suitable for auction. In terms of the second category above, the special purchaser may well be the only potential buyer, but he is much more likely to be reached by the extensive marketing of auction catalogues (one major firm regularly distributes over 12,000 catalogues) than by the limited exposure offered in a private treaty sale.

Although an auctioneer's ideal lot may be a good secondary parade of shops or secondary single shop investment, offices and industrial investments, together with development sites and ground rents, indeed virtually every type of commercial property may be suitable for auction. Not only are investments highly auctionable but so also are properties that are vacant, or with unusual reviews, or that are over-rented, or under-rented or even with deficit rents; properties with redevelopment potential, either short or long term; property with short life incomes, such as short leaseholds or short/medium term reversions; in fact, almost every type of property.

What the auction room still fails to attract is a substantial flow of prime investments. Only the institutions, with their unique concentration on long-term capital growth with maximum possible security and, of course, their tax-free status, can afford to pay prime yields. They have virtually inexhaustible funds for such investments and adopt a high profile in the market. A few letters or telephone calls offering such an investment for sale by private treaty is practically certain to produce an acceptable offer. The two-fold effect of this is that agents with prime instructions see no necessity to put such properties to auction, and that institutions are equally unlikely to consider auction as a method of sale for such properties. However, there are signs of change, as institutions question the validity of paying prime yields when improved techniques of portfolio analysis reveal insufficient growth to justify the yields paid. Institutions are increasingly turning towards secondary investments, where historical evidence suggests growth prospects are considerably higher on a 'value for money' basis.

The secondary market is a much wider field, defined at the extremes by good clean secondary investments on the one hand, and by 'difficult' or unusual investments on the other. The majority of secondary properties fall into neither of these categories but into a vast grey area in between. It is to these 'in-between' properties that the most important dual advantages of auction bring maximum benefit.

It is this grey area that causes the most headaches for the auctioneer, who has to assess the property's likely realisation for reserve purposes. Whilst he may be able to suggest a hypothetical yield, he cannot accurately assess the 'value' of the property without first ascertaining who are the potential buyers and on what basis they may make their possibly very different valuations. Although many people would say auctioning such properties removes the problem by letting the market decide the value, it is common practice for auction houses to quote guide prices. Too high a guide price will deter potential purchasers, whereas too low a price will win no friends for the auctioneer when the property is sold well in excess of what had been quoted. The accuracy of the guide price compared to the price actually achieved is usually a good indication of the skill and expertise of the auctioneer and his staff.

The Reserve

The auctioneer must also advise the vendor on the question of reserve, either before confirming instructions or just prior to the auction. In the latter case he has the considerable advantage of feedback from potential purchasers during the pre-auction marketing period. This can take the form of bids prior to the auction (although an auctioneer must be wary here – interested parties may make bids simply to 'test the water', trying in effect to discover the reserve or at least at what price the vendor would actually sell) or may simply be a question of ascertaining the amount of interest in a property. Both the vendor's solicitor and the joint auctioneer, if there is one, will also provide information as to the level of interest that may have been expressed. However high or low that level, the correct placing of the reserve is crucial to a successful sale. If the property is popular and is likely to attract a large number of bidders in the auction room, the reserve should be fixed at a level, say ten per cent, below the likely price achievable. This has the effect of letting the market know that the property is 'in the room', i.e. will be sold if no higher bid is received. Whether the auctioneer makes this explicit or not will depend upon the bidding. If it is slow, a suitable announcement from the rostrum will have the effect of stimulating renewed bidding. It is a regular feature of auctions that the auctioneer, when experiencing sluggish bidding for a property, will start his countdown to the fall of the gavel only to find (probably not to his surprise) that the room is suddenly full of higher bidders. Once it is clear that the property will be sold, open competition takes over and ferocious bidding can often follow, hopefully taking the price well above the reserve.

If, on the other hand, a property has attracted little or no interest, the reserve should be fixed close to the expected realisation in order to avoid selling at too low a price. Alternatively, but this is not for the faint-hearted vendor, the reserve can be disclosed at a low figure, low enough to attract sufficient buyers either to 'bid off the catalogue' (i.e. bid without first seeing the property) or to attract buyers to a property which they might otherwise have ignored, in the hope that a bargain may be had. Although the success of auctions depends on both satisfied vendors and satisfied purchasers the auctioneer must be constantly aware of the dangers of underselling a property. The real art of the auctioneer lies in fixing the reserve at a level which will encourage buyers who think they see a bargain and at the same time satisfy vendors that their properties are reaching the maximum price if there is only one bidder.

The Vendor

There are as many types of vendor at commercial auctions as there are types of property; they are usually selling for widely different reasons, and their needs differ accordingly. As in other property fields, they include receivers, trustees and others acting in a fiduciary capacity, central and local government and statutory authorities, and the Church. Particularly active in the commercial sector are private property companies, public property companies and institutions, and retail groups.

The Private Property Company An important source of commercial properties for sale by auction is the private property company, whose very nature requires it to sell regularly and realise capital gains (there are exceptions here in so far as some private property companies concentrate solely on high risk, high-yielding investments, where properties can be held for income on a largely self-financing basis – but these are undoubtedly in the minority). Such companies make their profits from general trading activities backed up by the relatively high yields obtained on secondary property, including the traditional break up of portfolios, improvement of property by restoration, development and subsequent sale.

More recently, active management has become increasingly important to property companies. This can take differing forms, but typically may involve buying in a freehold or negotiating a new lease in the case of leasehold investments, or negotiating surrenders and grants of new occupational leases, ideally for a long term or at an increased rent or to a better quality tenant, or with a more attractive review pattern, or with more acceptable repairing covenants – the possibilities are numerous for an imaginative entrepreneur.

♦ COMMERCIAL PROPERTY ♦

More simply it may involve just letting vacant space or negotiating an agreement for an advertising hoarding, or realising vacant possession value on residential accommodation above a shop through rehousing. Profitability depends most of all upon able management and imagination rather than upon inherent capital growth. Clearly the more successful the management, the higher the profit and, since the property crash of the early 1970s revealed the dangers of excessively high gearing, the only way to achieve this end is to implement a continuous programme of sales and new purchases. Auctions are ideally suited, because of the speed and neatness of the transaction and the fixed time-scale which, barring failure to achieve a sale, allows a company to plan ahead financially with a degree of certainty impossible if private treaty is used.

Another profit-making avenue open to the private property company is the straightforward 'turn', i.e. buying a property at what the purchaser considers to be an advantageous price and immediately reselling at a profit. Again the fixed time-scale of auctions is an obvious advantage, but more important to the buyer is the extensive marketing employed which will maximise his profit. Typically, a dealer will buy a property by private treaty, often through a provincial agent, and then immediately resell the property through a major London auction house.

The Public Property Company and Institutions Public property companies are also well-established vendors by auction, although generally for rather different reasons from the private sector. While some do concentrate on high yield, high risk investments, most concentrate primarily on development opportunities, which lead to auction sales in two ways. The first and more obvious of these occurs when a completed development is to be sold, either as a whole or by way of break up. The extent to which completed developments are subsequently sold or retained varies with the company and its need to produce a reasonable dividend yield, but, as mentioned, companies are now very wary of

♦ PROPERTY AUCTIONS ♦

excessively high gearing and are inclined to release profits for further investment whenever possible. The other aspect of development which produces suitable auction properties, results from the simple fact that by no means all proposed developments are actually carried out. In the current climate, developers will usually try to assemble most of their proposed development sites before publicly announcing their scheme. If at any stage of the proceedings the proposals are blocked, through planning problems, or public objections or inability to assemble a sufficient proportion of the earmarked sites, the company will be left holding a number of properties which it might well not otherwise have purchased. In such circumstances auction is an ideal method of disposing of these surplus properties.

Development aside, public property companies may also find themselves holding surplus properties as a result of wholesale acquisitions in the form of either portfolios or entire property companies. Rationalisation will be required and sale by auction will often be the most suitable method of achieving it. Public property companies and institutions will also wish to dispose of properties by way of auction as a result of under-performance. This is a problem which has been increasingly acute for the major financial institutions and is probably the main reason why they sell by auction.

Both public property companies and institutions identify as performing unsatisfactorily the type of property which is seriously affected by a change in the requirements of potential occupiers. A typical example would be a 1960s office building, originally let to a prime covenant and valued using a prime or near prime yield. With the advent of modern technology, particularly in the field of communications and data handling, tenant requirements have changed, so that such a building, on becoming vacant, would probably never command such a covenant again, and in some cases may even be completely unlettable in its current state. The situation is exacerbated by the fact that, with a typical twenty-five-year lease, the reversion may be imminent. There may also be other problems – high alumina cement or the use of woodwool slabs, for instance, or unfashionable lease terms, such as insufficiently tightly drafted repairing covenants or unattractively high gearing in the case of leasehold properties. Any combination of these problems can move a property from the prime to the secondary category with a dramatic effect on yield (the significant yield gap between prime and secondary properties has been referred to as 'the black hole').

Sometimes the building can be rescued by large-scale refurbishment, but even with this option the risks may be too high for both public property companies and institutions. The alternative is to sell to a private property company, who may be prepared to undertake the refurbishment or to use their expertise in active management to let the building in small suites to secondary tenants or to restructure a head lease or occupational lease. The vendor will gain maximum benefit from the diversity of approaches adopted by these private property companies and their consequent diversity in valuation techniques, if he sells by auction.

Retail Groups The major retail groups can also be an important source of auction properties. Particularly in more secondary locations these retailers may have acquired the freehold or long leasehold interest in their shops only to find some years later that they no longer suit their current requirements. This may be because the trading pitch has declined to an uneconomic level, possibly owing to the opening of a new supermarket or other shopping scheme, or to changes in transport routes, or it may simply be a question of the availability of a better location. The unit itself may no longer be suitable, possibly because of inadequate floor space, or insufficient car parking. Alternatively, units may become surplus as a result of a streamlining policy, possibly necessitated by falling profits. In many of these cases, of course, the retailer, having made the decision to go, will wish to sell the freehold or long leasehold with vacant possession as soon as possible. Auction in this instance may not necessarily be appropriate, since its very speed tends

♦ PROPERTY AUCTIONS ♦

to work against the possibly inexperienced potential owner-occupier who may require more time for arranging a loan, legal work and surveys. Furthermore, finding a potential owner-occupier generally requires more specific promotion than the auction's mass marketing techniques, which are likely to be wasted. One popular option open to the retailer, however, is to let the unit and then sell on the created investment. Many auction properties are of this type.

The other main way in which retailers can sell property at auction is by sale and leaseback. This is normally done in order to release capital, and as such may be employed by the owner of the local corner shop, just as easily as by the big conglomerate. It has also been done successfully by owners of industrial and office premises, although this is less common.

The Future

The growth in commercial auctions over the last decade has been dramatic. Inroads made into the private treaty market, once the sole domain of the 'investment surveyor' are likely to be permanent. The commercial auctioneer can now expect to put together a catalogue of between a hundred and three hundred lots and to have some six to eight hundred buyers at a sale, held over one or two days, in a central London venue. Some would argue that this is a short-term boom which cannot last, but the increasing body of satisfied purchasers would dispute this. The advantages of sale by auction are considerable and the disadvantages few and far between. The question is not 'how long will the "boom" last?' but 'how large a share of the market will the auction capture before an equilibrium is reached?'

· 7 ·

Industrial Property

Christopher Drury

In auction terms industrial property was the poor relation of its retail and residential cousins. Today, with industrial investments yielding high returns, there are indications that such properties could achieve a new level of popularity. This chapter considers the position of industrial property in the auction market principally as an investment. It also looks at the various matters requiring special attention when preparing the marketing campaign, and looks ahead to consider the auction potential of industrial property.

The Industrial Investment

The mid-1980s have brought strong indications that industrial investments are creating their own following. For example, certain firms found that the number of industrial properties offered for sale in 1985 and 1986 increased fourfold by comparison with the previous two years, with a highly successful sales rate.

There are logical reasons to explain the current popularity of industrial investments. The yield range for secondary industrials has risen from between 8% (for the better calibre) and 13%+ (for the poorer) in the early 1980s up to 11% and 16%+ for the equivalent in 1986. Indeed, investments yielding 20% and higher have not been uncommon. During the same period the return from long-dated gilts was slightly lower, while the cost of borrowing (clearing bank rates for lending) dropped significantly. Therefore the ability of rental income to cover the interest payments payable under mortgage borrowings improved significantly.

At the same time, there has been greater pressure on fund managers to achieve a satisfactory performance from their portfolio. Industrial properties purchased as modern investments during the 1970s and early 1980s at rates as low as seven per cent have been valued at eleven per cent in 1987. Even if the property has shown reasonable rental growth (and in the 1980s that has been a forlorn hope), the overall performance is likely to have been poor. Faced with the threat of vacant units as leases end or tenants succumb to the recession, and having a greater awareness of the effect of functional and physical obsolescence, fund managers have found themselves called upon to weed out non-performers.

Although it has been a painful process, vendors have begun to accept that if the secondary industrial element of their portfolio is to be sold, then high yields must be proffered to attract bidders. Hitherto the yield expectation gap between vendor and purchaser was difficult to bridge. But industrial investments now offer the prospect of higher yields than those derived from other forms of property investment. The effect of this shift in yield expectations has been to launch a large stock of property into a pool in which the dealer and high-yield investor thrive. Traditionally, such buyers are the backbone of property auction sales.

Furthermore, a new breed of purchaser for secondary industrial investments is emerging – the entrepreneurial fund manager who is breaking with the belief that a yield in excess of seven per cent should never be trusted; he is looking for a high return today with the possibility of more tomorrow, either in terms of rental growth or redevelopment potential, possibly for a more profitable purpose, e.g. 'high-tech' or retail warehousing or even residential development. The important feature of this new breed of fund manager is that he is prepared to bid at auction.

The auction market is well suited to secondary industrial investment property and the experience of the mid-eighties

◆ INDUSTRIAL PROPERTY ◆

has shown that two particular categories of industrial investment appeal most readily:

Category A

Location	– south-east within easy reach of the motorway network (particularly M25 or M4) or near one of the main airports
Age of building	– relatively immaterial providing it is functional and in reasonable repair
Tenant	– relatively immaterial
Lease	– likely to expire within 10 years
Yield	– 10-13%
Lot size	– £250,000-2m
Special characteristic	– the value of the site alone (i.e. ignoring the buildings standing on it) substantially underpins the value of the investment

Category B

Location	– virtually anywhere
Age of building	– reasonably modern (less than 15 years old)
Tenant	– sound covenant status
Lease	– 15 years + unexpired, ideally much longer
Yield	– 13% +
Lot size	– £250,000-1m

Two examples of typical properties in the first category sold at auction in the mid-1980s are:

1. Factory premises prominently located on an industrial estate near Gatwick Airport. The 1960s building occupied a site of about 1.1 acres and was let for a term having 12 years unexpired, produced an income of £51,000 p.a., subject to review 2½ years later when some uplift was expected. The property achieved a price of £575,000, reflecting an initial yield of about 8% and a relatively keen equivalent yield for an elderly industrial unit. The price, however, was

underpinned by the market's opinion of the potential development value of the site.

2. An estate of 13 light industrial/warehouse units in Hemel Hempstead producing a total income of about £160,000 p.a. with the majority of leases expiring in 1988. The estate sold at auction at a figure of about £1.25m suggesting an initial yield of about 12%; it was purchased by a major pension fund.

The essential ingredient of category A is the quality of location. Such properties are recognised as virtually self-funding land banks, and appeal to property companies and certain institutions.

The most significant feature of category B is the quality of tenant, linked with the high yield; such properties are relatively mortgageable and, therefore, are popular with smaller investors and property companies as well as dealers. An example of a category B property would be an industrial building in Gateshead; let to a major company for a term of 35 years from 1976, the property produced an income of £31,500 p.a. subject to review in 1997 only. The investment was knocked down in 1985 at a price reflecting a yield of about 14½%.

Properties lacking the essential ingredients outlined above under categories A and B expect compensation to be reflected in the yield which may typically fall within the 13-17% range although, unlike a certain well-known lager, even *Parry's Valuation Tables* do not reach the yield extremities appropriate for certain such investments! An example is a Victorian single-storey mill in Greater Manchester, on a lease having 11 years unexpired, at a rent of £56,000 p.a., achieving a price at auction in the mid-eighties of £262,000 (about 25%). The building was unoccupied and, in its existing form, was never likely to be otherwise. The investment value rested substantially on the perceived ability of the tenant to continue to pay the rent or the possibility of doing a deal with the tenant who might wish to buy himself off the hook. Despite the shortcomings of the premises, the auction generated considerable interest with bidders including at least one pension fund manager.

The Vacant Building

Vacant industrial buildings present a more difficult challenge to the auctioneer than their investment counterparts, which are more straightforward to categorise; this is not entirely surprising as in the former case the market will view the same property from different standpoints. A prospective owner-occupier (if there is one in the market at the time) may be prepared to bid more keenly than an investor seeking to buy the property and then having to find a tenant, thereby creating an investment. Unless the property is in a particularly depressed area, therefore, vendors usually try either to effect a letting themselves before offering the property on the market, or to find an owner-occupier. To offer a vacant industrial property for sale at auction may be construed by the market as signalling that a forced sale exists. For example, a modern freehold factory of some 40,000 sq. ft. in Manchester was offered for sale with vacant possession at auction at a realistic reserve. The property was to be sold on behalf of mortgagees who accepted the problems; in the event, no acceptable bid was forthcoming and the property was withdrawn. Some months later two potential owner-occupiers were found and competition between them drove the price to a figure of forty per cent higher than would have been acceptable at the time of the auction.

However the failure of vacant factories to sell under the hammer in areas particularly hit by the recession, should not be construed as reflecting badly on auctions as a method of sale. Such properties would be just as difficult to sell by private treaty, although the latter method does provide scope for patience, a vital ingredient in some cases. But it is essential that the auctioneer recognises the problems likely to be encountered and fully appraises his client accordingly. In difficult areas of the country, the advice should be, find a tenant first or be prepared to accept 'scrap' value; otherwise the vendor must expect a long wait for his or her price.

♦ PROPERTY AUCTIONS ♦

Thus, in 1984 an extensive factory in the north-east was offered for sale. Of the 430,000 sq. ft. only about 50,000 were occupied and producing income. The investment was sold at £175,000 reflecting a yield of 15% from the let section, the remainder of the accommodation being effectively 'thrown in'.

It would be wrong to assume that all vacant industrial properties fall into the 'difficult' category. Small self-contained units standing within their own site can prove an attractive commodity for some companies. There is an allure for many to own the freehold of their own premises, free of rental obligations (and the threat of reviews) and landlord interference. Pre-arranged mortgage finance can assist the purchase, and units under £100,000 in value can prove rewarding auction stock, particularly in the south-east. Similarly, small vacant warehouse units located close to a town's shopping or commercial centre may attract considerable attention from retailers or other large space occupiers nearby seeking accommodation as a back-up to service their principal premises.

Preparation for Auction of Industrial Property

Selling industrial property by auction is little different in essence from selling any other product: it has to be suitably presented. The need to anticipate the information likely to be required by potential purchasers is paramount; this is a consideration to bear in mind when inspecting the property and making other local enquiries. Without wishing to provide an exhaustive list the following information should be obtained for inclusion in the draft text or for holding in anticipation of enquiries from prospective purchasers.

At the Property The age of the building, its construction and floor areas, eaves height, provision of parking and the site cover, are all standard requirements for industrial property. Easier to overlook is the actual use to which the building is being put (does it comply with the planning regulations?). Boundaries should be checked on site against

♦ INDUSTRIAL PROPERTY ♦

information provided on plans, together with obvious easements and rights of way. Any factors which might inhibit redevelopment should also be noted.

The property should be looked at from the point of view of a potential buyer; it can be discouraging to uncover the drawbacks, but it is better to be prepared than put on the spot by purchasers' pre-auction enquiries or, worse, questions asked on the day. A critical look at the property during inspection can pay dividends when it comes to discussing the reserve with the vendor.

A property of poor appearance reflects badly, and possibly unfairly, on not only the condition of the building, but also the quality of the tenant. Where appropriate, advice should be given to the vendors as to how the property might be better presented. More often than not this may be done at the tenant's cost as part of his obligations under the lease although the implications in terms of time of serving a schedule of dilapidations will need to be considered; a less formal approach may be appropriate. A record of the state of landscaping, condition of the building or possible breaches of conditions of the lease (e.g. storing in the open) is important.

The name of the tenant actually occupying the building should be noted – is it the same as the name on the lease? The names of occupiers of adjoining units and major occupiers in the vicinity – each are possible special purchasers – should be recorded. Ownership of estate roads also needs to be established; if private, their condition should be recorded and precise ownership and repairing obligations checked.

At the Planning Office   The statutory register is essential reading. The permitted use of the property should be checked – light industrial (Class B1), general industrial (Class B2) or warehouse i.e. storage and distribution (Class B8). In some cases this may have little impact on value, but in certain areas of the country the implications may be more significant, particularly since the advent of the amendments to the Use Classes Order; these came into force in 1987 and merged light industrial use with office use to create a new business class (B1). This could create greater opportunities for light industrial premises.

Information which might be helpful to the marketing campaign can also be readily obtained at the local authority offices, for example, any proposed changes to the road system, the policy towards further industrial/warehouse development, the attitude towards 'high-tech' schemes (in some areas this might be particularly significant as far as site value is concerned), and any local or development plans which affect the site.

Potential Purchasers

Industrial investments are ideal fodder for those seeking a high initial return. Not only the smaller property company and dealer but increasingly the institutional investors are taking an interest in such investments. For companies also acquiring or holding lower yielding properties, the relatively high return from the industrial element provides a balance which can assist borrowing requirements. Any industrial investment with redevelopment potential should be mailed to development companies including, where appropriate, residential developers.

The Future

There seems little reason why industrial property should not continue to grow in popularity; such investments particularly cater for those purchasers seeking really high yields. Many couple this virtue with security of income derived from a tenant offering a sound covenant status. It is possible that other opportunities may be seized upon by the market.

Terraces of Units Arguably the one type of property which attracts interest more than any other is a parade of shops (see previous chapter). This appeals not only to the investor but also to the dealer who can break up the parade by selling off the shops individually. Possibly a terrace of industrial or warehouse units could attract similar attention, though the

♦ INDUSTRIAL PROPERTY ♦

exercise could be rather more complicated as there are likely to be communal areas (landscaped parts, car parking) or estate roads which are unadopted. This could involve the establishment of management companies or the disposal of individual units on long leases with the freeholder retaining control of the estate overall.

Retail Warehouses It is arguable whether such properties qualify for inclusion in this chapter, particularly since the new Use Classes Order (1987) specifically changes the old class 'warehousing' to 'storage and distribution' in order to make clear that retail warehouses – where the main purpose is the sale of goods direct to visiting members of the public – will generally fall within the shops class, whatever the extent of floor space used for storage. However, such properties attract considerable interest across the market, institutions, pension funds and property companies, included. As investments, retail warehouses offer respectable yields (8-9% on average), invariably strong tenant covenant, modern buildings, a prominent location, good landscaping and a stake in what is perceived as a future shopping trend. The ingredients of successful auction material must surely be present although such properties have not commonly been found in catalogues.

Nursery Units In the early eighties, a vast number of such schemes were developed to take advantage of the industrial development allowances. These developments are beginning to age and are no longer fashionable. Yield expectations have risen to a level which appeals to the secondary market. As the supply of new schemes dries up, tenant demand could continue to drive up rents, and the opportunity for break-up attract buyers, to the extent that it would be reasonable to foresee nursery unit schemes becoming popular auction stock.

· 8 ·

Land, Agriculture and Sporting

J. P. H. Wiseman FRICS, *of Michelmore Hughes*

The information given in this chapter is based on experience in the South-West of England, where there is a long history of all types of property being sold regularly by public auction. There are auction posters dating back to the early 1850s and bound property auction books from the 1870s, while one small printer still uses late eighteenth-century auction poster type and an 1875 printing press.

Traditionally, agricultural properties are sold by local firms, with assistance when required from national agents, as the most important factor for a successful auction of agricultural properties is local knowledge. This is something which is unlikely to be found in the London or regional office of a national agent, unless that office is directly involved in the area's business on a day-to-day basis.

The auction is usually conducted within striking distance of the subject property, and whilst attended mainly by local people (most of whom have no intention of buying the property but come along to see what the farm or land will fetch), serious purchasers from further afield will travel down in order to bid, for unlike the commercial property market, which is centred mainly on London, buyers of agricultural properties come from all parts of the UK.

♦ LAND, AGRICULTURE AND SPORTING ♦

SCOPE AND NATURE OF AGRICULTURAL AND COUNTRY PROPERTIES

A much greater variety of types of property is auctioned in the agricultural than in the residential market. At the lower end of the scale, a sale might involve a two- to three-acre pony paddock with a sale price of £4,000-9,000, offered at public auction in a local pub one evening, with a solicitor reading out the Special Conditions of Sale. At the top end, there may be a traditional agricultural estate, coming on to the market for the first time in three hundred years, and offered for sale as a whole or in lots, and sold in front of four to five hundred people in a nearby town hall, for a sum in excess of a million pounds.

Agricultural Estates These range from, for example, a small estate of about 120 acres including a large house, several staff and other cottages, a small farm, in-hand or let, surrounding the house, and possibly some fishing rights in a well-known fishing river adjoining, to a larger estate of 1,300 acres or more, consisting of a listed country house with several staff cottages, adjoining land of 15-20 acres, an in-hand or let farm of some 320 acres surrounding the house, several vacant lodges, two tenanted farms each of 250 acres, a few let cottages in the village, possibly a pub which is let, also in the village, about 250 acres of commercial woodland planted up since the war, a further 250 acres of woodland let on a 999-year lease to the Forestry Commission, two or three miles of double bank salmon and sea-trout fishing in a well-known fishing river which intersects the estate, parcels of accommodation land, and some sporting rights over adjoining land, which previously belonged to the estate but which was sold off with the sporting rights reserved to the estate. This type of property might be offered for sale as a whole or as, say, fifteen to twenty lots. It is important of course that each lot is saleable, so that everything is sold on the auction date.

Farms These can be either let or vacant. The auction market

◆ PROPERTY AUCTIONS ◆

for let farms, apart from farms sold as individual lots in an estate sale, is very thin since the most likely purchaser for a let farm will be the sitting tenant. It is, therefore, usual to sell these farms by private treaty, unless there are other reasons for offering the property for sale by public auction, for instance, an executor's sale where the residual beneficiary is a charity.

Vacant farms may be anything from a smallholding, possibly consisting of a bungalow subject to an agricultural planning restriction, with thirty acres, to a residential and commercial farm, with a good house, a secondary farmhouse, several cottages, a comprehensive collection of traditional and modern buildings, and land extending up to, say, five hundred acres or more.

Accommodation Land This might be a small pony paddock or a large block of bare agricultural land with no buildings (or possibly an off-lying set of buildings), up to about a hundred and fifty acres, such land normally being offered for sale in lots.

Moorland This can be large tracts of open moor subject to common rights, extending to, say, four thousand acres or more, likely to be purchased by commoners or graziers, or by private individuals who want to own a large area of cheap land.

Building Land This could either be an individual building plot, suited to a private purchaser, or several plots of interest to a local builder, or a good stretch of building land which might attract a national builder.

Sporting Rights These are mainly fishing rights and include salmon and sea-trout or trout fishing; they can extend from several fishing pools, up to two- or three-mile tracts of double bank fishing. Occasionally, sporting rights, which have been reserved out of the sale of agricultural land or farms, are offered for sale separately by public auction, but it is more common for these rights, unless part of an agricultural estate, to be sold by private treaty, as the owner of the

◆ LAND, AGRICULTURE AND SPORTING ◆

farm subject to the sporting reservation is usually keen to buy in what could otherwise be a considerable nuisance to him.

The easiest types of rural property to sell by public auction are residential investments, country cottages for modernisation, period vicarages, commercial investments which tempt the private investor, and individual building plots and barns suitable for conversion into dwelling houses. Quite often the only difficulty from the auctioneer's point of view is to record the bids fast enough. Furthermore, the preparatory work for these is comparatively straightforward, and an auction date can usually be arranged within five to six weeks of accepting instructions. Experience in this type of work is, however, all-important, and thus it is usually best undertaken by agents who regularly sell property by public auction.

TYPES OF CLIENTS AND THEIR NEEDS

Vendors

Trustees As explained in earlier chapters, trustees may be either professional trustees such as a solicitor, a bank or accountant, or lay trustees, who tend to require a more personal service. The auctioneer must bear in mind that the reason why they have instructed him to sell the property by auction is in order to convert value into cash. If the property does not sell the instructing trustees will not be happy. It is, therefore, up to the auctioneer to do whatever is necessary to stage-manage the affair from the time the instructions are accepted to the fall of the auctioneer's hammer, to be certain that the property is sold at its market price.

Professional trustees, whilst being as anxious as their lay colleagues to realise a sale, require paperwork to be kept to a minimum with the auctioneer accepting total responsibility for particulars, plans and conditions of sale. Lay trustees prefer to have paper evidence of the auctioneer's efforts on their behalf. All trustees however expect firm guidance and

◆ PROPERTY AUCTIONS ◆

recommendations from the auctioneer and demand a very high standard of expertise in order to ensure that they do not come under attack from the beneficiaries. Any auctioneer, therefore, whose advice is equivocal will soon run into difficulties.

Farmers and Landowners They are usually more demanding than trustees, and from the auctioneer's point of view often less amiable as they may well have taken other professional advice, which conflicts with the auctioneer's, e.g. from a bank manager or solicitor. In any event they require a comprehensive and personal service involving them closely in the preparation and marketing of the property.

It is important, in their case, for the auctioneer to identify the reason for the sale. If the vendor is on the point of insolvency, it is usually prudent to confirm instructions on a sole selling basis, in case the vendor is bailed out by a friend who buys part or all of the farm with the vendor remaining in possession.

Local and Public Authorities Their requirements are similar to trustees' but more time has to be allowed for the preparation of the auction before the property is launched on the open market. Generally, these clients are able to offer the auctioneer a greater level of professional support, once they are in a position to proceed.

Buyers

These include owner-occupiers, investors, dealers and developers. For the better agricultural property it is the local buyer who tends to bid the most at public auction rather than the buyer from farther afield. Usually the local purchaser will keep a low profile so as not to prejudice his position, and if enquiries have to be made beforehand he will employ another local auctioneer or solicitor to act on his behalf. The outsider will require more information from the auctioners and will, as mentioned above, do best to seek advice from a local rather than a national agent to achieve a successful purchase.

◆ LAND, AGRICULTURE AND SPORTING ◆

ADVANTAGE OF AUCTIONS OF RURAL PROPERTY FOR THE VENDOR

As with the other types of property dealt with in this book, the main benefit of an auction to a vendor is that it is one of the fastest ways of converting value into cash. There is no better way of disposing of an agricultural or sporting property which is generally available for sale than taking it to public auction.

In the case of a lotted sale for a farm or an estate, an auction is the only practical way of selling. The simultaneous exchange of contracts due to the fall of the auctioneer's hammer on each lot avoids the numerous problems of a gradually fragmenting and reducing property which will inevitably result from the sale of individual lots by private treaty.

AGENTS

Should the vendor instruct a local or a national agent? This question, which has already been touched on (see p. 78), always causes considerable debate. Should a national agent perhaps act in conjunction with the local one, or the national agent instruct a local one, or should the vendor instruct both a local and a national agent?

With traditional estates, it is probably best to instruct both a local and a national firm to act for them so that the full market potential is exploited. It is usually sensible for the local agent to appoint the national one since he will generally know which agents are currently most appropriate to a particular assignment. If an owner wishes to instruct a particular national agent, he should probably confirm instructions with that national agent on the basis that they also instruct a local firm, otherwise the property may not sell at auction. If an owner favours two local firms they can be instructed to act as joint auctioneers.

With farms, it is advisable for the owner to instruct only a local agent to sell unless it has outstanding residential appeal

◆ PROPERTY AUCTIONS ◆

and is in a sought-after area, in which case consideration might be given to instructing both a local and a national agent on the same basis as for a traditional agricultural estate. Farms can, of course, be advertised and marketed nationally by local agents. But the marketing campaign must be gauged according to the likely purchaser and not so as to further the prestige of the auctioneers. There is nothing worse than a farm which is obviously suited to a local purchaser being given the same marketing treatment (glossy printed brochures and extensive national advertising mainly in publications other than the farming press), as one would expect for a high quality residential farm in a fashionable part of the country. Quite aside from the added expense of this (which will be paid for by the vendor), the likely purchaser for this sort of farm will probably keep his head down and await developments and the failure of the farm to sell at auction.

ASSEMBLING THE AUCTION

The Preliminary Instruction and Sale Report

Once the preliminary instruction has been received a sale report should be prepared after going over the estate or farm in some detail. For a farm auction a short report would be adequate, but for a traditional estate a comprehensive report is necessary and should include:

The Brief Although this may seem obvious, it is important to confirm with the instructing client that the object of the report is to give detailed advice on the sale of the estate or farm with a view to obtaining the highest realisation figure. The client must be told the cost of the sale.

Method of Sale This should include advice as to whether the farm or estate should be sold in lots or as a whole, or marketed on a 'whole or lots' basis, and should explain the recommendation to sell by public auction rather than by other means. These decisions can be crucial. As an example, when two West Country farms running together failed to sell by private treaty through national agents, they were remarketed for auction, one of the farms being offered as a whole, the other divided into six lots, the traditional farm buildings having planning consent for conversion to residential use, and everything was sold either prior to or at auction, for around £900,000 (in 1985).

Recommendations for the various lots should be shown in a schedule or an appendix to the sale report and also on a plan attached to the report, giving reasons where appropriate. Advice should also be given as to whether the sporting and fishing rights should be sold with each respective lot or offered separately.

Appendices to the Sale Report   These might include:

Appendix A Schedule of Lots: listing the lots, with a brief description, the name of the tenant, the colour of the lot on the plan and the appropriate acreage.
Appendix B Schedule of Private Treaty Sales.
Appendix C Sale Plan, showing the individual lots in different colours.

Planning

Consultations should take place with the local planning authority, before or after preparation of the sale report, and, if appropriate, planning applications should be submitted so that the planning situation and any development potential on the estate is resolved before the auction date.

Timing and Promotion

It is essential that any property is placed on the market at the most beneficial time. Most agricultural properties look their best during May and June, so, all things being equal, an auction date towards the end of June is ideal. The date for completion must also be advised on, and with a June or early July auction date a late September (Michaelmas) completion will suit most vendors as well as the purchaser.

Photographs should be professionally taken the previous autumn, before the leaves come off the trees, otherwise

♦ PROPERTY AUCTIONS ♦

winter shots will have to be used and these, apart from being less attractive, do not print so well because of the dull light.

The instructing client should also be advised to keep the sale confidential until the property is launched on the open market, as very often an element of surprise is helpful in encouraging the competition necessary to ensure a sale at the highest possible level.

Once announced, the pending sale of a good farm or an estate will inevitably arouse great interest and it is important to encourage this in the hopes of obtaining the highest possible price by a wide publicity campaign using the following tools.

Auction Brochure   For a large agricultural estate this should be illustrated as necessary, and include a detailed plan and Conditions of Sale. For most farms, an illustrated printed brochure cover, incorporating a separate printed sale plan and photocopied sale particulars and Conditions of Sale, are adequate and save considerably on printing costs and time.

Advertising   Recommendations as to which local and national publications should be given to the vendor.

Press Release   A press release should be prepared and issued to local and national publications.

'For Sale' Boards   These should be erected in prominent positions on the more important road frontages enjoyed by the estate or farm.

Preparation of the Particulars

If the estate is being sold on behalf of trustees and there are a number of beneficiaries involved, the trustees may wish the auctioneers to attend a meeting with the beneficiaries so that the contents of the report can be discussed.

Once instructions have been confirmed a start can be made on preparatory work. The approximate lead times and various activities for an auction of an agricultural estate in mid-June would be:

♦ LAND, AGRICULTURE AND SPORTING ♦

October   Preparation and submission of sale report and photographs.

December   Meeting with trustees and beneficiaries to discuss the sale report, following which, it is hoped, instructions are given to proceed in accordance with its recommendations.

December-January   Property inspections should be made; these need to be efficient and thorough so that each property has only to be inspected once. A team of three is ideal – one to do the writing and two the measuring – one of whom should ask the occupier about:

1. Rights of way and access – if the property does not have a frontage to a public road; is it subject to rights of way in favour of an adjoining property;
2. Water supply – private or mains, and the route of the supply pipe from the natural source or the water authority main;
3. Drainage from buildings – main or private, and the location of the main sewer, the septic tank, cesspit or own disposal system;
4. Electricity and telephone;
5. Boundaries and their ownership.

The information retrieved from these enquiries (rights of way, encroachments by a third party, any other easements, the routes of the public services) must be set down, and a record made of those rights of way and easements to be granted or reserved in respect of the lots. It is usually advisable to have a separate water plan prepared showing the position of underground water pipes serving the various properties and field troughs.

A list of the items claimed by the tenant as his improvements or fixtures should be prepared, and if the property is going to be sold vacant, any items which the occupier proposes removing prior to completion should be noted; this is more likely in farms and cottages.

Farmland and woodland should be inspected to revise the Ordnance Survey maps, often necessary where an estate has

♦ PROPERTY AUCTIONS ♦

not come on to the market for some thirty years, and essential to the sale plan for a lotted sale since it will form part of the contract. The inspection is also the basis of the detailed valuation and schedules of acreages.

Informal enquiries should be made of the highway and local authorities in respect of public rights of way and public roads. It is surprising how many green lanes are in fact public roads. Formal enquiries should be made of the water authority, electricity board, British Telecom and regional gas board as to the location of their apparatus on the estate to confirm or correct what was mapped out after the inspection. Tenancy agreements and leases must be read.

Before the auction particulars are drafted, certain decisions will have to be made for farms sold with vacant possession. There will need to be an ingoing valuation which will stipulate that, in addition to the purchase price, the purchaser will pay at valuation for:

1. all unconsumed hay, straw and silage left on the holding;
2. all cultivations, seeds, sprays and artificial manure applied on the arable land since the last crop was harvested;
3. all growing crops of roots, such as swedes and kale;
4. all new grass seeds;
5. all stocks of fuel, oil, seeds, artificial manure and sprays left on the holding.

A valuation for milking and other fixed equipment, for grain drying equipment, grain storage bins and EEC quotas, will also have to be made unless these items are included in the purchase price.

Pre-entry and holdover rights must be established, pre-entry permitting the purchaser reasonable access to the arable land before completion in order to carry out after-harvest cultivations and to plant winter corn, and holdover being the right of entry and holdover for the vendor to allow him to harvest, for instance, a late spring corn crop, potatoes or

◆ LAND, AGRICULTURE AND SPORTING ◆

roots, after completion, and, sometimes, to use the grain store and associated handling and drying equipment free of charge (except for the cost of the electricity) during the winter following a Michaelmas completion.

Information should be sought from the accountants as to the unexpired portion of capital allowances under Section 68 of the Capital Allowance Act 1968, as the benefit of this passes to the purchaser.

A draft of the auction particulars in so far as his farm is concerned should be sent to each farm tenant for comment.

A draft sale plan showing the individual lotting should be prepared and the original Ordnance Survey sheets should be amended, preferably by the auctioneers using their own artwork, as this saves time for the printer and on proofing the plans. A schedule of acreages should be prepared giving a description for each Ordnance Survey number.

Detailed notes should be prepared on each lot covering: rights of way and access, water, drainage, electricity and telephone, and fencing, to be incorporated in the Special Conditions of Sale. Other items may be included, if appropriate, such as the ingoing valuation; pre-entry, holdover, auction sales of livestock and deadstock; tenancy; sporting rights if reserved; tree preservation orders; Forestry Commission Dedication agreements; Ancient Monuments and Sites of Special Scientific Interest. Planning matters, such as agricultural planning restrictions, Listed Buildings and Article 4 Directions (Town and Country Planning General Development Order 1977, whereby a planning authority can restrict certain General Development Order permitted development rights, such as to erect fencing or certain sized agricultural buildings, and make them subject to individual planning permission) will also need to be covered.

End of January These detailed stipulations and notes should be used to brief the vendor's solicitors so that they can draw up the Special Conditions of Sale without having to refer back for instructions. If it is a complicated lotted sale, the solicitors need to be shown the relevant lots on the ground,

◆ PROPERTY AUCTIONS ◆

and they should be given a draft of the sale plan, a schedule of acreages and a draft of the auction particulars. The solicitors should also be given a set of auction particulars from a previous sale so that they can incorporate stipulations applicable to all lots. They should then be allowed, depending on the size and complexity of the estate, at least a month in which to draft the conditions.

Their draft, when received, will need checking thoroughly; it may run to some sixty typed pages, and owing to the diverse nature of property, may easily contain inaccuracies. But the Special Conditions of Sale must be correct, otherwise the auctioneers are open to criticism not only from the instructing client but also from the prospective purchasers and their solicitors, all of whom consider, in the case of an agricultural estate and most farms, that the auctioneers are entirely responsible for the satisfactory conduct of the sale. The complexity of a large agricultural estate being sold in lots is such that it would be quite impossible for a solicitor, in the time available to him, to consider and specify, for example, all the necessary easements and rights of way to be reserved and granted.

The solicitors should also be asked to forward to the auctioneers copies of the current local search and duplicate copies of all the documents referred to in the Special Conditions of Sale so that one set is always available for serious purchasers on a perusal and return basis. As it may be impractical to copy a large number of duplicate conveyances, the vendor's solicitors should provide space for prospective purchasers or their solicitors to examine these documents at their offices.

March Drafts of the auction particulars and sale plan should go to the printer, along with a draft of the Special Conditions of Sale, though the latter can be fitted in quite well at a later date if necessary. Inevitably, two or three stages of proofs will be required as the particulars will have to be amended in view of further details or developments; but it is important, from the point of view of cost, that printing is

◆ LAND, AGRICULTURE AND SPORTING ◆

done during business hours and not in the evenings or at weekends when charges go up enormously. Whatever happens, the final draft of the brochure needs to be ready for distribution when the sale is announced. If there are then revisionary notices to the particulars or to the Conditions of Sale, these can be issued from the rostrum at the time of the sale.

Price guides need agreeing for the individual lots and national advertising should be booked.

April-Early May Once the estate has been launched on the market the printed brochure can be sent to all on the mailing list and the sale boards erected. The auction is then ready to proceed as normal.

THE COUNTRY AUCTIONEER

Finally, a word on the qualifications and experience needed by the country auctioneer. Ideally, an auctioneer of agricultural property should be a chartered surveyor and a full member of the Central Association of Agricultural Valuers. He should have on-the-spot local knowledge of agricultural matters. Thus, most auctioneers of agricultural property are either land agents or agricultural auctioneers with livestock markets, or estate agents specialising in the sale of farms rather than in country houses with the occasional farm.

More often than not auctioneers of agricultural properties will also be selling all other types of property on behalf of their firms by public auction on a regular basis. Prior to conducting his first property auction, it is usually best for an auctioneer to gain adequate experience of selling other items by this means. Ideally, any potential property auctioneer should be selling property by public auction as a senior professional assistant in his mid- to late-twenties, so that by the time he is a partner he is no longer a novice.

· 9 ·

Conduct Unbecoming

Clive Carpenter

The purpose of this chapter is not to delve too deeply into the legislation encompassing the field of auctioneering but to explore the effect of what it imposes upon the conduct of auctions, for auctioneers, vendors and purchasers, in both legal and moral terms, i.e. the chapter will attempt to determine those practices which are justified and those which are not. Anyone who is contemplating taking up the gavel would also be well advised to obtain a copy of the excellent work entitled *Auctions: Law and Practice* by Brian Harvey and Frank Meisel, published by Butterworth in 1985; also highly recommended is J. R. Murdoch's *The Law of Estate Agency and Auctions* (Estates Gazette, 2nd ed., 1984).

STATUTES DIRECTLY AFFECTING THE SALE OF PROPERTY BY AUCTION

Sale of Land by Auction Act 1867

This Act (see p. 145) attempted, albeit unsuccessfully, to resolve the conflict between common law and equity, whereby, provided that the right of the vendor or his agent to bid is reserved, then the vendor or his agent can bid on his behalf. Unfortunately the Act is silent as to whether this right to bid, if properly reserved, should be up to the reserve only or above. The shortcomings of this Act are discussed below.

♦ CONDUCT UNBECOMING ♦

Auctions (Bidding Agreements) Act 1927 and 1969

These Acts (see pp. 146-9) specifically attempted to prevent auction 'rings', but the definition of 'dealers', the only people to whom the Acts apply, as 'a person who in the normal course of his business attends sales by auction for the purpose of purchasing goods with a view to reselling them', arguably limits their application to chattel auctions. Nonetheless, a copy of them has to be exhibited in some conspicuous part of the auction room or place where the auction is held, just as the auctioneer's full name and address must be, these latter details as stipulated by the Auctioneers Act 1845 (see p. 145).

Auction rings comprise a group of persons who conspire together not to bid so as to allow one member of the ring to acquire a property on behalf of the ring at a lesser amount than would otherwise have been paid had all the members participated individually in the bidding. A second auction or 'knock-out' is usually held amongst the ring members afterwards.

The problem that an auctioneer or vendor faces is proving that a ring existed at the time of sale. The very nature of a ring's operation is secretive. However, in 1981 and 1983, successful prosecutions were instigated by the police. In the former case the detectives involved caught members of a ring red-handed on a beach in southern Wales dividing the spoils of their ill-gotten gains; in the latter, similar proceedings were filmed by the police in the bar of a hotel. No other successful prosecutions have been brought under these Acts. It would presumably be even harder to gain sufficient evidence in the event of a real estate auction ring being suspected as no goods would change hands. At the same time, it would be virtually impossible for a ring to operate in a modern property auction room with several hundred people present of various nationalities.

◆ PROPERTY AUCTIONS ◆

Misrepresentation Act 1967 (pp. 149–50)

A purchaser who can prove that, as a result of a misrepresentation made by the auctioneer or his staff, he has suffered loss, can issue proceedings against the vendor who may join in the auctioneer in such proceedings. Further, if as a breach of warranty of authority, such misrepresentation has been made without authority from the vendor, the auctioneer may be liable to both the vendor and the purchaser. Practising auctioneers are therefore advised to be very careful to ensure that any statements made, whether orally or in writing, are accurate.

Exemption clauses excluding liability for such misrepresentation are only effective if they satisfy the requirement of reasonableness (see below on the Unfair Contract Terms Act 1977). In the case of *South Western General Property Co Ltd v. Marton* (1982) 263 EG 1090, for instance, the purchaser sought to rescind the contract despite numerous exemption clauses, including a clause stating that the auctioneers had no authority to make or give any representation or warranty concerning the property, a plot of land, and won against the vendor on the grounds that none of the exemption clauses satisfied the reasonableness requirement.

Theft Act 1968

Messrs Harvey and Meisel suggest that the auctioneer could by taking bids 'off the wall' be held to be obtaining property, which for the purposes of this Act includes money, by deception. To date no auctioneer has been prosecuted under this Act, but the practice or malpractice of taking bids 'off the wall' is discussed further below (pp. 97-9).

Unfair Contract Terms Act 1977

This Act (see pp. 150-2) is of relevance to all three parties to an auction, the vendor, the purchaser and the auctioneer, since it applies to any clauses intending to limit or exclude liability, such clauses having effect only if they satisfy the statutory test of reasonableness (see Schedule 2 of the Act,

p. 152). It is the responsibility of the party claiming protection from the clause to show that it is reasonable. This same test applies to clauses claiming to exclude liability for misrepresentation under the Misrepresentation Act (see above). It may be noted that Sections 2-4 of the Act, on avoiding liability for negligence and unreasonable indemnity clauses do not extend to 'any contract so far as it relates to the creation or transfer of an interest in land'.

Estate Agents Act 1979

Specifically aimed at controlling the activities of estate agents, this Act regulates estate agents and auctioneers' handling of deposits and any other clients' money held on trust by them (see pp. 153-5, below). The Act requires full disclosure by the auctioneer of any personal interest that he may have in property being sold by him. The provisions of the Act apply also to 'joint auctioneers' and, for example, to an agent who may introduce a property to an auctioneer acting in a joint capacity as such. (For full discussion of this Act, see J. Murdoch, idem., and his *The Estate Agents Act 1979*, Estates Gazette, 2nd ed., 1982).

THE AUCTIONEER'S CODE OF CONDUCT

It will be seen from the foregoing that there is comparatively little legislation directly affecting the activities of a property auctioneer. As the mysteries of the auction room publicly unfold, thanks to media coverage, and the public become more informed, it is hardly surprising that some will question the manner in which the unusual role of the auctioneer is played. The very power that the auctioneer exercises in effecting a contract on the fall of his gavel, is in itself unique. The way this authority is exercised should not only be legal but also, notwithstanding his prime duty to act with skill and care on behalf of his client, fair to the purchaser for whom he is also agent, albeit to a limited extent, at the moment the gavel falls, when he can sign in the name of and on behalf of the purchaser a memorandum of sale sufficient to satisfy the provisions of the Law of Property Act 1925, in so far as they relate to a sale of land (for sample memoranda of sale, see Appendix 5). If the legislative and contractual relationship between auctioneer and purchaser is slight (since contractual relations are essentially between purchaser and vendor), the auctioneer has a moral responsibility to the purchaser. The auctioneer who observes this responsibility will, as a result of the goodwill created, command a larger market-place. The practices, or rather malpractices, upon which prospective bidders need to be reassured, are as follows:

Unsold Lots

Throughout the post-war period, the practice of real estate auctioneering has been undertaken without attracting too much criticism of the auctioneer's conduct and it was only during the summer of 1985 that, as a result of the alleged malpractice of a well-known auction house, at a sale held in New York, that the public's attention was quite rightly focused on the activities of auctioneers in general. At the same time, although in no way related, a British television documentary highlighted some of the practices encouraged by a well-known firm of chattel auctioneers, and felt by many to be improper. The New York affair revolved around the practice by which some chattel auctioneers knocked down lots as sold and gave the impression that they were sold when they were not. The documentary, meanwhile, followed the path of a reporter being trained as a novice auctioneer and learning the procedure to be adopted when a lot failed to sell, namely, that the lot was always to be knocked down, thus indicating to the lay public that a sale had been achieved. Presumably by so doing, it was hoped to retain confidence in the market. Whilst both instances involved chattel auctioneers and the law relating to them differs in certain areas, the public may tend to class chattel and property auctioneers together.

There are several reasons why it is essential that the auctioneer conveys the truth to the market-place, as to when a property is sold or not. By purposely giving the impression that a property has achieved a certain value, it could well cause another buyer to suffer substantial loss as a result of the setting of an artificial value. For example, a purchaser, having relied upon the results of a sale, may be induced to pay more than he otherwise would have done for a comparable property. In the event of a resale, he would be quite likely to suffer financial loss. Further, both professionals and the courts have relied upon auction results as evidence of value, accepting them as true and accurate. If adopted by real estate auctioneers, such a malpractice would, above all others, bring the profession into grave disrepute.

Bidding 'Off the Wall'

The difficulty that a purchaser often experiences is that he cannot be sure that he is being treated fairly by the auctioneer when bidding in a room with several hundred people present. He needs to be reassured that those persons appearing to bid against him are actual purchasers and not figments of the auctioneer's imagination, conjured up to create an atmosphere of unfair competition.

The practice of some auctioneers of taking 'bids off the wall' is well-known to most professionals, but not necessarily to the lay market. It is entered into by some auctioneers either in order to create interest in a lot which otherwise may have none or as a technical device to enable the auctioneer to reach the reserve in instances where there is only one buyer. Among property auctioneers, the practice is contentious, some feeling that in their clients' interest it is justified, others not. Indeed some feel there could be an element of fraud in so doing and Messrs Harvey and Meisel in their book suggest that despite no one's having been prosecuted for taking bids 'off the wall', the auctioneer is potentially criminally liable. Two elements would have to be satisfied for a case to succeed, firstly, the practice would need to be regarded as dishonest by the ordinary standards of honest and reasonable people, and, secondly, the defendant auctioneer would have to appreciate that his conduct was so regarded. Furthermore,

♦ PROPERTY AUCTIONS ♦

the burden of proof would be upon the purchaser to show not only that the auctioneer had taken such fictitious bids, but also that he had acted fraudulently by so doing, a difficult burden of proof, as the auctioneer would quite rightly allege that the practice had been a 'custom of the trade' for a great many years and one that was supported by the Director-General of the Office of Fair Trading in a press statement of 29 October 1980.

Provided that the auctioneer is careful to observe Section 6 of the Sale of Land by Auction Act 1869 (see p. 146), the auctioneer can overcome his difficulty in reaching the reserve price in the event of there being only one buyer present. The auctioneer can bid on behalf of the vendor or, alternatively, the vendor can bid himself or through an agent, the latter commonly known as a 'puffer' and specifically referred to in Section 4 of the Act. It is contended that the Act allows only for the vendor *or* his agent to bid, since permitting more than one person to bid on the vendor's behalf could mislead a prospective purchaser into believing that the lot in question was in greater demand than it was. The judge in *Parfitt v. Jepson*, a case brought ten years after the Act, stated that in his view the Act had abolished altogether the practice of employing more than one 'puffer' so as to give the appearance of competition, in other words, taking bids 'off the wall'; while, in the little-known case of *Heakley v. Newton* (1881), it was held, though not as an issue in the case, that even when the conditions of the sale allowed the vendor to bid, if the auctioneer ran up a price by pretending to receive from various parts of the auction room bids which were not, in fact, made, the sale would not be upheld. It should be reasonable to assume that although over a hundred years have passed, a court would not take a different view.

Unfortunately, Sections 5 and 6 of the Act were so clumsily drafted that they have increased the confusion they were intended to prevent by failing to say how the vendor's bids could be made, i.e. whether they could be consecutive. It is submitted here that consecutive bids by the vendor or on his behalf can be made, provided the right to bid is properly reserved. The intention of the Act was not to place a vendor in a worse position than if he had decided to sell by private treaty, when he can repeatedly reject offers. When an auctioneer decides he might need to bid consecutively, he would best do so through a puffer, and if challenged, he could identify the latter as bidding for the vendor only, so, arguably, not creating an artificial atmosphere of competition. The validity of this contention has still however to stand the test of the courts. Notwithstanding, in 1987, a property auctioneer was challenged by a trading standards officer, following a complaint from someone at the sale, with taking bids 'off the wall', when he was in fact exercising his right to bid on behalf of the vendor, though not by consecutive bids, up to the reserve. Although the auctioneer had no case to answer, it seems that the Office of Fair Trading is taking a keener interest in the activities of auctioneers.

Price Guides

It is sometimes the custom of auctioneers to issue price guides to the market-place prior to a sale. When this is done conscientiously it can be of assistance to both the buyer and seller. However, notwithstanding the genuine difficulty in assessing the hammer price in advance without the aid of a crystal ball, there has been a tendency over recent years for some auctioneers to deflate purposely the estimates for specific lots. This has been done in order to attract the attention of prospective purchasers, who may unnecessarily incur considerable costs in assessing the lot for sale, to find that it is sold substantially in excess of the guide price given. The possible short-term gain cannot be condoned.

Lots Sold or Withdrawn Prior to Auction

Likewise, purchasers and their advisers can expend considerable sums only to find that the lot is sold or withdrawn prior to the auction. The practice of some auctioneers of failing to take the trouble to inform all parties who have expressed interest to them of such an event, leaves much to be desired.

♦ PROPERTY AUCTIONS ♦

Purchase and Sale of Lots by Interested Parties

In order to retain the auctioneer's absolute integrity, and to assure the vendor of the total impartiality of the auctioneer when conducting a sale, an auctioneer should not bid for himself or his family unless his client specifically agrees to this action prior to the sale. As mentioned above (see p. 95), any auctioneer contemplating the sale of property in which he has an interest, as defined by the Estate Agents Act 1979, should disclose such interest in accordance with the terms of that Act (see p. 155).

Auctioneers' Fees and the 'Buyer's Premium'

The practice of some chattel auctioneers of charging a 'buyer's premium' is deprecated by most property auctioneers. It is widely felt that to charge both parties is iniquitous. Indeed, some would say that by so doing, the auctioneer cannot act competently for his vendor client since he is also being paid by the purchaser. Whilst auctioneers do have duties and liabilities owed to the purchaser, as referred to above, they are not those that require payment. The auctioneer's most important duty is to the vendor; to ensure that he obtains the very best price and it is for this task that he is paid. This is in direct conflict with the interest of the purchaser, who will require to purchase a property at the least possible price. A dog cannot have two masters.

♦

In conclusion, whilst all auctioneers have statutory duties and liabilities to both vendor and purchaser, it is contended that the auctioneer owes the purchaser a moral duty to conduct the auction in such a manner as not to mislead him and to treat him fairly. A successful auctioneer commands both the goodwill of his vendor client and that of the purchaser. An auctioneer who ignores the interest of either, does so at his peril.

· 10 ·

The Future

Janice McKenzie

The auction world has had a chequered history and it used to have a somewhat shady reputation. This reputation has, by and large, improved, as have the personalities involved; and the future will be, to an extent, dictated by the current personalities and, more importantly, those who follow them. Auctioneering is a personal business and a client will often stick with one firm because he is happy with the 'personality' on the rostrum.

We have had a stable of auctioneers who have remained constant for the last few years – effectively since the real estate auction market took off again after the recession of the mid-seventies. These men, however, now have 'seconds' who are helping them out on the rostrum and who may eventually replace them. Those new faces will have to make their mark with a buying and selling public that can be loath to accept changes. Vendors are notorious for not wishing to entrust the sale of their property to an unknown.

Other changes will arise when any of the major auctioneers goes public or joins one of the conglomerates which have sprung up since deregulation of the Stock Exchange. Now that chartered surveyors are allowed to incorporate and become public companies without losing their chartered status, following the 1986 decision of the Royal Institution of Chartered Surveyors, auction departments may find themselves swallowed up by concerns with very different interests.

♦ PROPERTY AUCTIONS ♦

Several agencies have 'floated' and, in the auctions world, at least one firm has been absorbed by a house sales business. From being a fair-sized part of a small firm, the auctions department has become a small cog in a very big machine. Such a situation could put an auction department in the position whereby it might not be able to give the personal service so important in this field. In the event of an auctioneering firm 'going public', the priorities within that firm would change, as the former partnership would then be responsible to its shareholders and not purely to itself. Supposing a scandal hit such a firm? In the past it would have been possible for a partnership to have taken the heat out of the situation because of its private nature, but in the case of a public company the shareholders would have to be informed. This could lead to the firm pulling out of the auction business altogether.

As we saw in the Christie's scandal, where the then chairman of the firm in New York claimed pictures were sold when they were not, a market can be quite drastically altered by the conduct of one individual, although the art world seems quickly to have weathered the storm; but the real estate auctioneering world is still comparatively young. It was only in the mid-1980s that near prime property began to appear in auction catalogues. Parades of shops with good quality covenants now come under the hammer where previously the auction room was a place of last resort. If a Christie's-type scandal were uncovered in the property world, through the actions of just one of the practitioners, it could mean the demise of the auction method of sale. Guidance notes have been contemplated by the RICS to stop this and most of the major auctioneers, at least in London, are members of the Institution and insist that their staff are also members. In 1986, Westminster City Council, under whose auspices the London Auction Mart falls, introduced their own set of conditions regarding conduct. Although these seem designed more to protect the public from the wiles of itinerant chattels auctioneers and to ensure the physical safety of premises than to provide a code of conduct

◆ THE FUTURE ◆

for property auctioneers, all auction houses in Westminster are now required to be licensed and in the event of malpractice within a house the licence can be withdrawn to prevent the operation continuing. The London Auction Mart itself very discreetly issued guidance notes for its auctioneers early in 1987 concerning amongst other matters, realistic guide prices, the requirement that where the vendor (or his agent, who may be the auctioneer) has the right to bid up to the reserve it must be so stated in the Conditions of Sale, and accurate publication of results.

Most auctioneers think it undesirable for central government legislation to be introduced to cover auction practice. This would be a lengthy process and could well hamper the smooth running of auctions and be virtually impossible to enforce. A point perhaps not appreciated by the layman is that confidentiality on the part of auctioneers, vendors and buyers, is an integral part of the auction process. Neither vendors nor buyers want to be named and prefer not to be recognised, often going to great lengths to preserve their anonymity, even working through pre-arranged signals so as not to have names or initials divulged on the floor (see above, pp. 26-7). Any legislation could put this very special relationship in jeopardy.

The future of the auction sector will also depend on the overall state of the property market. The auction world is dominated by secondary property and any shift in investment criteria by, for example, the big institutions, could change it. The institutions and pension funds have devoted their property spending, which recent reports suggest is decreasing, to prime City offices, which show yields down to 4.5%, to prime shopping with yields of about 4.5% and, increasingly less, to prime industrials which produce yields of approximately 8%. At auction, secondary shops showed yields of between 7% and 10%, in 1987, industrials an average of about 14% and secondary office investments were acquired for between 8% and 14%, depending upon location, age, construction and covenant.

Some lone voices in the wilderness are suggesting that the

♦ PROPERTY AUCTIONS ♦

pension funds should look towards the secondary market for a more immediate return, especially with regard to the obsolescence factor in the office sector which, in today's rapidly moving market, is becoming an increasing problem (see chapter 6, on the failings, particularly, of 1960s office blocks). These voices point out that investing at, say, five per cent in offices will mean that by the time the capital spent is returned, the building will no longer be of any use, unless of course some refurbishment programme has been initiated. However, if a parade of shops is bought at ten per cent, the block will still have plenty of life left in it at the end of the ten-year span in which the capital is recouped.

If the institutions were to move in on the auction market, it could mean the squeezing out of the traditional dealers and small investors. But the institutions still seem to be wary of the auction market although many of the big funds, as well as property companies, are more than prepared to sell unwanted stock by that method.

The institutional interest in selling property has much to do with the very high prices recently being achieved at auction. Among the factors that will dictate whether this trend continues will be the continuing supply of mortgage money for purchases. The availability of mortgages in the mid-eighties is reflected in some firms having set up their own internal financial services divisions, offering loans of up to seventy-five per cent of the purchase price of any lot bought at their auctions.

At the same time, exceptionally high prices have been paid for house building land. The main source of the land has been the British Rail Property Board. A record £8.1m was achieved for a parcel of such land sold at auction in 1986. The future of this important sector of the auction market will depend on the availability of land to sell. The British Rail Property Board has largely exhausted its supply of extensive portions of land, although the availability of smaller lots has seen the Board using more locally-based agents, a policy which spells good news for the smaller operations outside London.

♦ THE FUTURE ♦

Shops still dominate the commercial auction world and this shows no sign of changing. It seems unlikely that offices will ever form a large part of the market although as current 'high-tech' buildings age, it will be interesting to see whether their owners will retain and refurbish these or use the auction method of sale and, indeed, if so, whether anyone will want to buy the units.

Demand for houses, whether tenanted or vacant or in whatever condition, seems to be insatiable although they are seldom held for investment purposes but are usually traded on. With this in mind it seems likely that this sector of the market will continue to flourish. However, if, the government successfully relaxes or abolishes the Rents Acts in order to encourage a private rented market, then this situation could alter quite dramatically. It would be much more attractive, in a freer market, for a buyer at auction to hold on to a tenanted house, in the hope of raising the rent to a true open market and economic level. Hitherto, such houses have been for 'hope value', i.e. with a view to achieving vacant possession, and prices paid reflect this.

The two most recent Conservative administrations, 1979-87, have permitted the property market to prosper. Free enterprise has been allowed to flourish, taxation has been cut and, as has been pointed out, there has been no shortage of credit. Auctions are a source of both income and employment. Income for the government comes from the taxation on profits made by firms who run auction departments and from stamp duty on property sales. There are secondary sources of income too – printing companies, for instance, make profits from the increasingly lavish catalogues produced by the auctioneers, while journals and newspapers find auctions a good source of advertising revenue. And because property auctions are so effective, obsolete and vacant buildings can be quickly sold, refurbished or redeveloped by the purchaser, and relet, thereby creating more employment.

The auction departments of the big firms have expanded considerably as the volume of business has increased. Some

◆ PROPERTY AUCTIONS ◆

firms could absorb the extra staffing if the auction market were to go into decline but it would not be so easy for others. For example, where any auction department is basically an offshoot of the investment department, as is often the case in the big agencies, it is likely that the staff involved with auctions could be absorbed. However, a firm which is heavily reliant on auctions for business might not find it so easy.

There are undoubtedly some firms that would continue to carry on their auction activities even if there were a decline in the market, albeit on a scaled-down basis. But an auction is a highly expensive operation to mount – some sources put the cost in six figures. The postage of the catalogue alone is daunting (see above, p. xiv). Nonetheless there have been some new players who have come on to the field in the mid-eighties, and they have scored some notable successes. For instance, an outer London firm has done well with vacant and tenanted houses on its home patch.

In Scotland, a firm started auctioneering again, after a gap of some years, in February 1984, thanks to the British Rail Property Board's increasing their auction activities. If and when the Board's supply dries up, it may be wondered whether the firm will continue to auction property, since it is a method of buying and selling that the Scots have found hard to accept.

So we are left with an auction market dominated by the south-east, with the London Auction Mart as the hub of the activity. Drastic changes in the nature of residential auctions in Great Britain seem unlikely, although there have been reports of an increasing number of individuals buying their homes at auction, particularly in the London salerooms. The dwindling stock of unmodernised flats and houses, with vacant possession, is most likely to turn up at auction, being sold by such respectable bodies as the Metropolitan Police and mortgage companies shedding their repossessions.

As well as the possibility of finance being obtained through the auctioneering firms (see above), the private auction buyer should find that the building societies are gearing their

◆ THE FUTURE ◆

services more to his needs. Eventually, the private purchaser should come to appreciate both the cheaper legal costs attached to buying by auction, since more are borne by the vendor, and the elimination of the long periods of waiting and uncertainty which are often the fate of the private treaty buyer (although some local authorities find it hard to handle searches in the time required). So the day may come when, instead of going to the local estate agent for a house, Jo Bloggs will go along to his nearest auction house and bid for his next property, as is done in Australia.

In conclusion, the auction market has altered considerably since the mid-1970s. Expansion, particularly between 1982 and 1987, has been enormous and shows no signs of abating, although there have been some casualties along the way. However, if the auctioneers who have contributed to and enjoyed this boom continue to dominate the sector, and, more importantly, pass on their wealth of knowledge and experience on the rostrum to those coming up, political and economic factors aparts, the auction market should continue in its healthy state.

Appendix 1

The National Conditions of Sale (20th Edition, 1981)

CONSTRUCTION OF THE CONDITIONS

In these conditions, where the context admits –
(1) The 'vendor' and the 'purchaser' include the persons deriving title under them respectively
(2) 'Purchase money' includes any sum to be paid for chattels, fittings or other separate items
(3) References to the 'Special Conditions' include references to the particulars of sale and to the provisions of the contract which is made by reference to the conditions
(4) The 'prescribed rate' means the agreed rate of interest or, if none, then the rate of interest prescribed from time to time under Land Compensation Act 1961, s. 32
(5) 'Solicitor' includes a barrister who is employed by a corporate body to carry out conveyancing on its behalf and is acting in the course of his employment
(6) 'Working day' means a day on which clearing banks in the City of London are (or would be but for a strike, lock-out, or other stoppage, affecting particular banks or banks generally) open during banking hours Except in condition 19(4), in which 'working day' means a day when the Land Registry is open to the public
(7) 'Clearing bank' means a bank which is a member of CHAPS and Town Clearing Company Limited
(8) The 'Planning Acts' means the enactments from time to time in force relating to town and country planning
(9) On a sale by private treaty references to the 'auctioneer' shall be read as references to the vendor's agent
(10) On a sale in lots, the conditions apply to each lot
(11) 'Abstract of title' means in relation to registered land such documents as the vendor is required by Land Registration Act 1925, s. 110, to furnish.

THE CONDITIONS

1. The Sale: by Auction: by Private Treaty
(1) Paragraphs (2) to (5) of this condition apply on a sale by auction and paragraphs (6) and (7) on a sale by private treaty
(2) Unless otherwise provided in the Special Conditions, the sale of the property and of each lot is subject to a reserve price and to a right for the vendor or any one person on behalf of the vendor to bid up to that price
(3) The auctioneer may refuse any bid and no person shall at any bid advance less than the amount fixed for that purpose by the auctioneer

(4) If any dispute arises respecting a bid, the auctioneer may determine the dispute or the property may, at the vendor's option, either be put up again at the last undisputed bid, or be withdrawn

(5) Subject to the foregoing provisions of this condition, the highest bidder shall be the purchaser and shall forthwith complete and sign the contract, the date of which shall be the date of the auction

(6) Where there is a draft contract, or an arrangement subject to contract, or a negotiation in which there are one or more outstanding items or suspensory matters (which prevent there being yet a concluded agreement of a contractual nature), a solicitor, who holds a document signed by his client in the form of a contract of sale in writing and embodying this condition, shall (unless the other party or his solicitor is informed to the contrary) have the authority of his client to conclude, by formal exchange of contracts, or by post, or by telex or other telegraphic means, or by telephone, and in any case with or without involving solicitors' undertakings, a binding contract in the terms of the document which his client has signed

(7) The date of the contract shall be –

(i) the date, if any, which is agreed and put on the contract, but if none, then

(ii) on an exchange of contracts by post (unless the parties' solicitors otherwise agree), the date on which the last part of the contract is posted, or

(iii) in any other case, the date on which, consistently with this condition, a binding contract is concluded.

2. Deposit

(1) Unless the Special Conditions otherwise provide, the purchaser shall on the date of the contract pay a deposit of 10 per cent. of the purchase price, on a sale by auction, to the auctioneer, or on a sale by private treaty, to the vendor's solicitor and, in either case, as stakeholder

(2) In case a cheque taken for the deposit (having been presented, and whether or not it has been re-presented) has not been honoured, then and on that account the vendor may elect –

either (i) to treat the contract as discharged by breach thereof on the purchaser's part

or (ii) to enforce payment of the deposit as a deposit, by suing on the cheque or otherwise.

3. Purchaser's Short Right to Rescind

(1) This condition shall have effect if the Special Conditions so provide, but not otherwise

(2) If the property is affected by any matter to which this condition applies, then the purchaser may by notice in writing (hereinafter referred to as a 'Condition 3 Notice') given to the vendor or his solicitor and expressly referring to this condition and the matter in question, and

notwithstanding any intermediate negotiation, rescind the contract on the same terms as if the purchaser had persisted in an objection to the title which the vendor was unable to remove

(3) A Condition 3 Notice shall not be given after the expiration of 16 working days from the date of the contract, time being of the essence of this condition

(4) This condition applies to any matter materially affecting the value of the property, other than –

(i) a matter which was not yet in existence or subsisting at the date of the contract

(ii) a specific matter to which the sale was expressly made subject, or

(iii) a matter of which the purchaser had at the date of the contract express notice or actual knowledge, not being notice or knowledge imputed to the purchaser by statute solely by reason of a registration of such matter, or notice or knowledge which the purchaser is only deemed to have had by the conditions

(5) This condition and condition 15 are additional to each other.

4. *Chattels, etc., and Separate Items*
If the sale includes chattels, fittings or other separate items, the vendor warrants that he is entitled to sell the same free from any charge, lien, burden, or adverse claim.

5. *Date and Manner of Completion*
(1) The completion date shall be the date specified for the purpose in the contract or, if none, the 26th working day after the date of the contract or the date of delivery of the abstract of title, whichever be the later

(2) Unless the Special Conditions otherwise provide, in respect of the completion date time shall not be of the essence of the contract, but this provision shall operate subject and without prejudice to –

(i) the provisions of condition 22 and

(ii) the rights of either party to recover from the other damages for delay in fulfilling his obligations under the contract

(3) The purchaser's obligations to pay money due on completion shall be discharged by one or more of the following methods –

(i) authorisation in writing to release a deposit held for the purposes of the contract by a stakeholder

(ii) banker's draft issued by a clearing bank

(iii) cheque drawn on and guaranteed by a clearing bank

(iv) telegraphic or other direct transfer (as requested or agreed to by the vendor's solicitor) to a particular bank or branch for the credit of a specified account

(v) legal tender

(vi) any other method requested or agreed to by the vendor's solicitor

(4) Completion shall be carried out, either formally at such office or place as the vendor's solicitor shall reasonably require, or (if the parties' solicitors

◆ APPENDICES ◆

so arrange) by post, or by means of solicitors' undertaking concerning the holding of documents or otherwise Provided that on a sale with vacant possession of the whole or part of the property, if the conveyance or transfer will not, by overreaching or otherwise, discharge the property from interests (if any) of persons in, or who may be in, actual occupation of the property or such part of it, then (subject always to the rights of the purchaser under Law of Property Act 1925, s. 42(1)), the purchaser may, by giving reasonable notice, require that on, or immediately before the time of, completion possession of the property or part be handed over to the purchaser or his representative at the property

(5) The date of actual completion shall be the day on which, the contract being completed in other respects the purchaser has discharged consistently with the provisions of this condition the obligations of the purchaser to pay the money due on completion Provided that–

(i) for the purposes only of conditions 6, 7 and 8, if but for this proviso the date of actual completion would be the last working day of a week (starting on Sunday) and the purchaser is unable or unwilling to complete before 2.15 p.m. on that day, then the date of actual completion shall be taken to be the first working day thereafter

(ii) a remittance sent by post or delivered by hand shall be treated as being made on the day on which it reaches the vendor's solicitor's office, unless that day is not a working day in which case the remittance shall be treated as being made on the first working day thereafter.

6. Rents, Outgoings and Apportionments
The purchase being completed (whether on the completion date or subsequently), the income and outgoings shall be apportioned as follows (the day itself in each case being apportioned to the vendor):
(1) In a case to which proviso (i) to condition 7(1) applies apportionment shall be made as at the date of actual completion
(2) In a case in which the purchaser is in possession of the whole of the property as lessee or tenant at a rent apportionment shall be made as at the date of actual completion unless proviso (ii) to condition 7(1) applies, when apportionment shall be made as at the date of the purchaser's notice under that proviso
(3) In any other case apportionment shall be made as from the completion date Provided nevertheless that, if delay is attributable to the vendor's failure to obtain the reversioner's licence, where necessary, or if the vendor remains in beneficial occupation of the property after the completion date, the purchaser may by notice in writing before actual completion elect that apportionment shall be made as at the date of actual completion
(4) Rates shall be apportioned according to the period for which they are intended to provide and rents (whether payable in advance or in arrear) according to the period in respect of which they have been paid or are payable; and apportionment of yearly items (whether or not the same are payable by equal quarterly, monthly or other instalments) shall be

according to the relevant number of days relatively to the number of days in the full year

(5) Service charges under leases, in the absence of known or readily ascertainable amounts, shall be apportioned according to the best estimate available at the time of completion and, unless otherwise agreed, the vendor and the purchaser shall be and remain mutually bound after completion to account for and pay or allow to each other, within 15 working days after being informed of the actual amounts as ascertained, any balances or excesses due.

7. *Interest*

(1) If the purchase shall not be completed on the completion date then (subject to the provisions of paragraph (2) of this condition) the purchaser shall pay interest on the remainder of his purchase money at the prescribed rate from that date until the purchase shall actually be completed Provided nevertheless–

  (i) That (without prejudice to the operation of proviso (ii) to this paragraph) the vendor may by notice in writing before actual completion elect to take the income of the property (less outgoings) up to the date of actual completion instead of interest as aforesaid

  (ii) That, if the delay arises from any cause other than the neglect or default of the purchaser, and if the purchaser (not being in occupation of the property in circumstances to which condition 8 applies) places the remainder of his purchase money (at his own risk) at interest on a deposit account in England or Wales with any clearing bank, and gives written notice thereof to the vendor or his solicitor, then in lieu of the interest or income payable to or receivable by the vendor as aforesaid, the vendor shall from the time of such notice be entitled to such interest only as is produced by such deposit

  (iii) That the vendor shall in no case be or become entitled in respect of the same period of time both to be paid interest and to enjoy income of the property, or to be paid interest more than once on the same sum of money

(2) The purchaser shall not be liable to pay interest under paragraph (1) of this condition–

  (i) so long as, or to the extent that, delay in completion is attributable to any act or default of the vendor or his mortgagee or Settled Land Act trustees

  (ii) in case the property is to be constructed or converted by the vendor, so long as the construction or conversion is unfinished.

8. *Occupation pending Completion*

(1) If the purchaser (not being already in occupation as lessee or tenant at a rent) is let into occupation of the property before the actual completion of the purchase, then, as from the date of his going into occupation and

◆ APPENDICES ◆

until actual completion, or until upon discharge or rescission of the contract he ceases to occupy the property, the purchaser shall–
    (i) be the licensee and not the tenant of the vendor
    (ii) pay interest on the remainder of the purchase money at the prescribed rate
    (iii) keep the property in as good repair and condition as it was in when he went into occupation
    (iv) pay, or otherwise indemnify the vendor against, all outgoings and expenses (including the cost of insurance) in respect of the property, the purchaser at the same time taking or being credited with the income of the property (if any)
    (v) not carry out any development within the meaning of the Planning Acts
(2) Upon discharge or rescission of the contract, or upon the expiration of 7 working days' or longer notice given by the vendor or his solicitor to the purchaser or his solicitor in that behalf, the purchaser shall forthwith give up the property in such repair and condition as aforesaid
(3) A purchaser going into occupation before completion shall not be deemed thereby to have accepted the vendor's title
(4) Where the purchaser is allowed access to the property for the purpose only of carrying out works or installations, the purchaser shall not be treated as being let into occupation within the meaning of this condition.

9. Abstract, Requisitions and Observations
(1) The vendor shall deliver the abstract of title not later than 11 working days after the date of the contract but, subject and without prejudice as mentioned in condition 5(2), that time limit shall not be of the essence of the contract
(2) Subject always to the rights of the purchaser under Law of Property Act 1925, s. 42(1), the vendor may be required by the purchaser to deal with requisitions and observations concerning persons who are or may be in occupation or actual occupation of the property, so as to satisfy the purchaser that the title is not, and that the purchaser will not be, prejudicially affected by any interests or claims of such persons.
(3) The purchaser shall deliver in writing his requisitions within 11 working days after delivery of the abstract, and his observations on the replies to the requisitions within 6 working days after delivery of the replies
(4) In respect of the delivery of requisitions and observations, time shall be of the essence of the contract, notwithstanding that the abstract may not have been delivered within due time
(5) The purchaser shall deliver his requisitions and observations on the abstract as delivered, whether it is a perfect or an imperfect abstract, but for the purposes of any requisitions or observations which could not be raised or made on the information contained in an imperfect abstract, time under paragraph (3) of this condition shall not start to run against the

purchaser, until the vendor has delivered the further abstract or information on which the requisition or observations arise
(6) Subject to his requisitions and observations, the purchaser shall be deemed to have accepted the title.

10. Vendor's Right to Rescind
(1) If the purchaser shall persist in any objection to the title which the vendor shall be unable or unwilling, on reasonable grounds, to remove, and shall not withdraw the same within 10 working days of being required so to do, the vendor may, subject to the purchaser's rights under Law of Property Act 1925, ss. 42 and 125, by notice in writing to the purchaser or his solicitor, and notwithstanding any intermediate negotiation or litigation, rescind the contract
(2) Upon such rescission the vendor shall return the deposit, but without interest, costs of investigating title or other compensation or payment, and the purchaser shall return the abstract and other papers furnished to him.

11. Existing Leaseholds
(1) Where the interest sold is leasehold for the residue of an existing term the following provisions of this condition shall apply
(2) The lease or underlease or a copy thereof having been made available, the purchaser (whether he has inspected the same or not) shall be deemed to have bought with full notice of the contents thereof
(3) On production of a receipt for the last payment due for rent under the lease or underlease, the purchaser shall assume without proof that the person giving the receipt, though not the original lessor, is the reversioner expectant on the said lease or underlease or his duly authorised agent
(4) No objection shall be taken on account of the covenants in an underlease not corresponding with the covenants in any superior lease
(5) The sale is subject to the reversioner's licence being obtained, where necessary. The purchaser supplying such information and references, if any, as may reasonably be required of him, the vendor will use his best endeavours to obtain such licence and will pay the fee for the same. But if the licence cannot be obtained, the vendor may rescind the contract on the same terms as if the purchaser had persisted in an objection to the title which the vendor was unable to remove
(6) Where the property comprises part only of the property comprised in a lease or underlease, the rent, covenants and conditions shall, if the purchaser so requires, be legally apportioned at his expense, but completion shall not be delayed on that account and in the meantime the apportionment by the auctioneer shall be accepted, or the property may at the option of the vendor be sub-demised for the residue of the term, less one day, at a rent apportioned by the auctioneer and subject to the purchaser executing a counterpart containing covenants and provisions corresponding to those contained in the lease or underlease aforesaid

◆ APPENDICES ◆

(7) Any statutory covenant to be implied in the conveyance on the part of a vendor shall be so limited as not to affect him with liability for a subsisting breach of any covenant or condition concerning the state or condition of the property, of which state and condition the purchaser is by paragraph (3) of condition 13 deemed to have full notice, and where Land Registration Act 1925, s. 24, applies the purchaser, if required, will join in requesting that an appropriate entry be made in the register.

12. *Vendor's Duty to Produce Documents*

(1) If an abstracted document refers to any plan material to the description of the property, or to any covenants contained in a document earlier in date than the document with which the title commences, and such plan or earlier document is in the possession or power of the vendor or his trustees or mortgagee, the vendor shall supply a copy thereof with the abstract

(2) If the property is sold subject to restrictive covenants, the deed imposing those covenants or a copy thereof having been made available, the purchaser (whether he has inspected the same or not) shall be deemed to have purchased with full knowledge thereof

(3) The vendor shall not be required to procure the production of any document not in his possession or not in the possession of his mortgagee or trustees, and of which the vendor cannot obtain production, or to trace or state who has the possession of the same.

13. *Identity: Boundaries: Condition of Property*

(1) The purchaser shall admit the identity of the property with that comprised in the muniments offered by the vendor as the title thereto upon the evidence afforded by the descriptions contained in such muniments, and of a statutory declaration, to be made (if required) at the purchaser's expense, that the property has been enjoyed according to the title for at least twelve years

(2) The vendor shall not be bound to show any title to boundaries, fences, ditches, hedges or walls, or to distinguish parts of the property held under different titles further than he may be able to do from information in his possession

(3) The purchaser shall be deemed to buy with full notice in all respects of the actual state and condition of the property and, save where it is to be constructed or converted by the vendor, shall take the property as it is.

14. *Property Sold Subject to Easements, etc.*

Without prejudice to the duty of the vendor to disclose all latent easements and latent liabilities known to the vendor to affect the property, the property is sold subject to any rights of way and water, rights of common, and other rights, easements, quasi-easements, liabilities and public rights affecting the same.

◆ PROPERTY AUCTIONS ◆

15. Town and Country Planning
(1) In this condition, where the context admits, references to 'authorised use' are references to 'established use', or to use for which permission has been granted under the Planning Acts, or to use for which permission is not required under those Acts, as the case may be
(2) The purchaser shall be entitled to deliver, with his requisitions in respect of the title, requisitions concerning the authorised use of the property for the purposes of the Planning Acts. The vendor in reply shall give all such relevant information as may be in his possession or power
(3) Where the property is in the Special Conditions expressed to be sold on the footing of an authorised use which is specified, then if it appears before actual completion of the purchase that the specified use is not an authorised use of the property for the purposes of the Planning Acts, the purchaser may by notice in writing rescind the contract, and thereupon paragraph (2) of condition 10 shall apply. But, subject to the foregoing provisions of this condition, the purchaser shall be deemed to have accepted that the specified use is an authorised use of the property for the purposes of the Planning Acts
(4) Save as mentioned in the Special Conditions, the property is not to the knowledge of the vendor subject to any charge, notice, order, restriction, agreement or other matter arising under the Planning Acts, but (without prejudice to any right of the purchaser to rescind the contract under paragraph (3) of this condition) the property is sold subject to any such charges, notices, orders, restrictions, agreements and matters affecting the interest sold
(5) Subject as hereinbefore provided, and without prejudice to the obligations of the vendor to supply information as aforesaid, the purchaser shall be deemed to buy with knowledge in all respects of the authorised use of the property for the purposes of the Planning Acts.

16. Requirements by Local Authority
(1) If after the date of the contract any requirement in respect of the property be made against the vendor by any local authority, the purchaser shall comply with the same at his own expense, and indemnify the vendor in respect thereof: in so far as the purchaser shall fail to comply with such requirement, the vendor may comply with the same wholly or in part and any money so expended by the vendor shall be repaid by the purchaser on completion
(2) The vendor shall upon receiving notice of any such requirement forthwith inform the purchaser thereof.

17. Errors, Mis-statements or Omissions
(1) Without prejudice to any express right of either party, or to any right of the purchaser in reliance on Law of Property Act 1969, s. 24, to rescind the contract before completion and subject to the provisions of paragraph (2) of this condition, no error, mis-statement or omission in any prelimi-

◆ APPENDICES ◆

nary answer concerning the property, or in the sale plan or the Special Conditions shall annul the sale, nor (save where the error, mis-statement or omission relates to a matter materially affecting the description or value of the property) shall any damages be payable, or compensation allowed by either party, in respect thereof

(2) Paragraph (1) of this condition shall not apply to any error, mis-statement or omission which is recklessly or fraudulently made, or to any matter or thing by which the purchaser is prevented from getting substantially what he contracted to buy

(3) In this condition a 'preliminary answer' means and includes any statement made by or on behalf of the vendor to the purchaser or his agents or advisers, whether in answer to formal preliminary enquiries or otherwise, before the purchaser entered into the contract.

18. Leases and Tenancies

(1) Abstracts or copies of the leases or agreements (if in writing) under which the tenants hold having been made available, the purchaser (whether he has inspected the same or not) shall be deemed to have notice of and shall take subject to the terms of all the existing tenancies and the rights of the tenants, whether arising during the continuance or after the expiration thereof, and such notice shall not be affected by any partial or incomplete statement in the Special Conditions with reference to the tenancies, and no objection shall be taken on account of there not being an agreement in writing with any tenant

(2) Where a lease or tenancy affects the property sold and other property, the property sold will be conveyed with the benefit of the apportioned rent (if any) mentioned in the Special Conditions or (if not so mentioned) fixed by the auctioneer, and no objection shall be taken on the ground that the consent of the tenant has not been obtained to the apportionment and the purchaser shall not require the rent to be legally apportioned

(3) The purchaser shall keep the vendor indemnified against all claims by the tenant for compensation or otherwise, except in respect of a tenancy which expires or is determined on or before the completion date or in respect of an obligation which ought to have been discharged before the date of the contract

(4) Land in the occupation of the vendor is sold subject to the right (hereby reserved to him) to be paid a fair price for tillages, off-going and other allowances as if he were an outgoing tenant who had entered into occupation of the land after 1st March 1948, and as if the purchaser were the landlord, and in case of dispute such price shall be fixed by the valuation of a valuer, to be nominated in case the parties differ by the President of the Royal Institution of Chartered Surveyors.

19. Preparation of Conveyance: Priority Notices: Indemnities

(1) Where the interest sold is leasehold for a term of years to be granted by the vendor, the lease or underlease and counterpart shall be prepared

by the vendor's solicitor in accordance (as nearly as the circumstances admit) with a form or draft annexed to the contract or otherwise sufficiently identified by the signatures of the parties or their solicitors
(2) In any other case the conveyance shall be prepared by the purchaser or his solicitor and the following provisions of this condition shall apply
(3) The draft conveyance shall be delivered at the office of the vendor's solicitor at least 6 working days before the completion date and the engrossment for execution by the vendor and other necessary parties (if any) shall be left at the said office within 3 working days after the draft has been returned to the purchaser approved on behalf of the vendor and other necessary parties (if any)
(4) Where the property is unregistered land not in an area of compulsory registration and the conveyance is to contain restrictive covenants, and the purchaser intends contemporaneously with the conveyance to execute a mortgage or conveyance to a third party, he shall inform the vendor of his intention and, if necessary, allow the vendor to give a priority notice for the registration of the intended covenants at least 15 working days before the contract is completed
(5) Where the property is sold subject to legal incumbrances, the purchaser shall covenant to indemnify the vendor against actions and claims in respect of them; and the purchaser will not make any claim on account of increased expense caused by the concurrence of any legal incumbrancer
(6) Where the property is sold subject to stipulations, or restrictive or other covenants, and breach thereof would expose the vendor to liability, the purchaser shall covenant to observe and perform the same and to indemnify the vendor against actions and claims in respect thereof
(7) Paragraphs (5) and (6) of this condition shall have effect without prejudice to the provisions of Law of Property Act 1925, s. 77, and Land Registration Act 1925, s. 24, where such provisions respectively are applicable, and in respect of matters covered by a covenant implied under either of those sections no express covenant shall be required.

20. Severance of Properties formerly in Common Ownership
Where the property and any adjacent or neighbouring property have hitherto been in common ownership, the purchaser shall not become entitled to any right to light or air over or in respect of any adjacent or neighbouring property which is retained by the vendor and the conveyance shall, if the vendor so requires, reserve to him such easements and rights as would become appurtenant to such last-mentioned property by implication of law, if the vendor had sold it to another purchaser at the same time as he has sold the property to the purchaser.

21. Insurance
(1) With respect to any policy of insurance maintained by the vendor in respect of damage to or destruction of the property, the vendor shall not (save pursuant to an obligation to a third party) be bound to keep such

◆ APPENDICES ◆

insurance on foot or to give notice to the purchaser of any premium being or becoming due

(2) The purchaser shall be entitled to inspect the policy at any time

(3) The vendor shall, if required, by and at the expense of the purchaser obtain or consent to an endorsement of notice of the purchaser's interest on the policy, and in such case the vendor (keeping the policy on foot) may require the purchaser to pay on completion a proportionate part of the premium from the date of the contract.

22. *Special Notice to Complete*

(1) At any time on or after the completion date, either party, being ready and willing to fulfil his own outstanding obligations under the contract, may (without prejudice to any other right or remedy available to him) give to the other party or his solicitor notice in writing requiring completion of the contract in conformity with this condition

(2) Upon service of such notice as aforesaid it shall become and be a term of the contract, in respect of which time shall be of the essence thereof, that the party to whom the notice is given shall complete the contract within 16 working days after service of the notice (exclusive of the day of service): but this condition shall operate without prejudice to any right of either party to rescind the contract in the meantime

(3) In case the purchaser refuses or fails to complete in conformity with this condition, then (without prejudice to any other right or remedy available to the vendor) the purchaser's deposit may be forfeited (unless the court otherwise directs) and, if the vendor resells the property within twelve months of the expiration of the said period of 16 working days, he shall be entitled (upon crediting the deposit) to recover from the purchaser hereunder the amount of any loss occasioned to the vendor by expenses of or incidental to such resale, or by diminution in the price.

THE CONDITIONS ARE REPRODUCED BY KIND PERMISSION OF THE SOLICITORS' LAW STATIONERY SOCIETY PLC.

Appendix 2

General Conditions of Sale

THESE CONDITIONS OF SALE ARE USED BY A LEADING FIRM FOR THEIR AUCTIONS OF COMMERCIAL PROPERTY

1. The Properties are sold subject to the following Conditions and to the Conditions known as the National Conditions of Sale (20th Edition) except that:

(i) Condition 4, 12(1), 15(2) and 15(3) thereof shall not apply and the words 'no bid shall be withdrawn' shall be added to the end of Condition 1(3);

(ii) Condition 7(1) shall be read as though the words 'remainder of his' had been deleted;

(iii) The proviso to Condition 7(1) shall not have effect and if the purchaser shall not be completed on the completion date referred to then (subject to the provisions of paragraph (2) of the said Condition) the Vendor shall be entitled to be paid both interest on the remainder of the purchase money and to receive any income from the property. If interest becomes payable in accordance with Condition 7 and the Vendor is in occupation of the property the Vendor shall in no case be obliged to pay any occupational rent in respect thereof.

In the event of any conflict between the National Conditions of Sale and these General Conditions then the General Conditions shall prevail. In the event of any conflict between these General Conditions and the Special Conditions in respect of a particular property then the Special Conditions shall prevail. A copy of the said National Conditions may be inspected at the offices of the auctioneers or of the solicitors for the Vendors as stated in the Particulars hereto on any day during business hours and in the Sale Room at or immediately before the sale and each purchaser shall be deemed to have knowledge of all the provisions.

2. Unless otherwise stated, the sale is subject to a reserve price for each of the properties and the Vendors reserve the right to bid themselves or through their agents at the Auction.

3. A deposit of 10% of the purchase price shall be paid to the Auctioneers, . . . as Stakeholders.

4. The Auctioneer reserves the right to regulate the bidding and to refuse to accept any or all bids without assigning any reason therefore in his sole absolute discretion. In the event of any dispute on bidding the Auctioneer's decision shall be final.

5. The tenure of the respective properties and the estate or interest sold are as stated in the relevant particulars and/or Special Conditions of Sale. In the case of any property where the the title is registered at H.M. Land

♦ APPENDICES ♦

Registry the title shall be deduced and consist of a copy of the entries on the Register and the filed plan and an authority to inspect the Register. In the case of any property where the title is not so registered it shall be deduced as provided by the Special Conditions.

6. The National Conditions of Sale shall be read and construed as if the rate of interest referred to therein were 5% per annum above National Westminster Bank PLC base rate for the time being but with a minimum of 16% per annum.

7. The Purchaser of any lot or part being a leasehold interest shall within three days of the date hereof supply to the Vendor's Solicitors satisfactory reference to enable the Vendor to apply for a licence to assign where this is necessary.

8. The completion date shall be:
   (a) in the case of freehold property 28 days after the date on which the Contract of Sale is made;
   (b) in the case of a leasehold property the later of:
   (i) 28 days after the date on which the Contract of Sale is made or
   (ii) the first working day after the expiration of three days from the date on which the Vendor shall have obtained the reversioner's licence in accordance with National Condition 11 of the National Conditions of Sale (20th Edition). If the reversioner's licence shall not have been obtained within three months of the date on which the Contract of Sale is made, the Vendor may rescind the contract on the same terms as if the Purchaser had persisted in an objection to the title which the Vendor was unable to remove.

9. The Purchaser shall be deemed to have made local land charge searches and enquiries of the relevant local and other authorities and entities and have knowledge of all matters that would be disclosed thereby and shall purchase subject to all such matters.

10. The Purchaser shall be responsible for complying with any schedule of dilapidations which shall be served either before or after the date of the sale.

11. The properties are believed and shall be taken to be correctly described as to quantity and otherwise and any error, omission or misstatement found in the Particulars or Conditions shall not annul the sale or entitle the Purchaser to any compensation in respect thereof. The Auctioneers shall be under no financial liability in respect of any matters arising out of the auction or the Particulars or Conditions of Sale.

12. In case any cheque given as a deposit shall be dishonoured upon presentation or a Purchaser fails to pay a deposit on acceptance, then without notice a Vendor shall if he so chooses, have the right to deem the conduct of such Purchaser as a repudiation of the contract and the Vendor may resell without notice and/or take steps which may be available to him as a consequence of a Purchaser's breach but without prejudice to

♦ PROPERTY AUCTIONS ♦

any claim he may have against the purchaser for breach of contract or otherwise.

13. The properties are sold subject to any existing tenancies, leases, agreements or licences referred to in the Particulars of Sale and/or Special Conditions of Sale. Whether or not the Purchasers shall have inspected any leases, counterpart leases, tenancies and other matters subject to which a property is sold, they shall be deemed to purchase with full knowledge of the contents thereof and shall make no objection or raise any requisition with respect thereto, notwithstanding any partial, incomplete or inaccurate statement thereof in the Particulars, nor shall any objection be taken to the absence of any agreement in writing with any occupier.

14. (1) No representation is made that the rent payable in respect of any property or part thereof sold subject to a tenancy is properly chargeable under the Rent Act 1977 or previous Rent Acts or similar legislation or any substituted or other statute for the time being in force regulating the control of rents or that the landlord was entitled to obtain possession at the time when any notice increasing rent under the said Acts became operative. The only representation made or intended or implied by or from the relevant particulars is that the amounts so stated are the respective rents actually reserved to the Vendors and no objection or requisition shall be taken or made as to any matter arising under the said legislation or any legislation for the time being amending or replacing the same or any other statute or legislation whatsoever. No Purchaser shall be entitled to require particulars of the standard rent or the limit or of the net rent or of the fair rent or the present or former regulated rent payable in respect of any of the properties or any part thereof nor to the production of copies of statutory notices of increase of rent and notices to quit (if any) which have been served. No Purchaser shall raise any objection that any relevant property has not at any time been registered with the local authority as decontrolled and no Purchaser shall require any particulars which under the said Acts or any rules made thereunder are to be inserted in the tenants' rent books to be so inserted nor require to be supplied with any particulars for insertion. In the case of a regulated tenancy, no objection, requisition or enquiry shall be made on the ground that the same is not a fair rent or that the same may exceed the registered rent under the appropriate legislation or that the same (if applicable) has not been registered. No objection shall be taken by a Purchaser as to whether or not a notice of increase of rent has or has not been validly served or as to whether or not a certificate of disrepair has been obtained by a tenant authorising a reduction of rent, nor shall any purchaser object to or claim damage or compensation or rescission on the ground that the Vendors have not complied with the terms of any counter notice served upon or by a tenant. Neither the Vendors nor the Auctioneers shall be under any duty to acquaint Purchasers of any such matters, whether or not the same are known to the Vendors or the Auctioneers and the Purchasers shall in all respects

◆ APPENDICES ◆

satisfy themselves at their own risk and whether or not they do so, no claim shall be made or entertained on the grounds that the Purchaser should have been informed of any such matters and the Purchasers shall be deemed to have full knowledge of all matters relating to the properties under the provisions of the Housing Acts or Rent Acts or any similar legislation or any statutory amendment or re-enactment thereof and shall raise no objection or requisition whatsoever thereon.

(2) If at the date of completion there should be any tenants in the relevant property who are in arrears with their rent the relevant Purchaser shall pay to the relevant Vendors the full amount of such arrears due on the date of actual completion and such Vendor will if required by such Purchaser assign to him the arrears due from the tenant to the Vendor, the cost of preparing arranging and executing such assignment being borne by the Purchaser.

15. Each Purchaser shall satisfy himself as to ownership of electric wiring and fittings and/or gas fittings and installations in the property sold as in some cases the same are on hire or hire purchase from the relevant supply company. Neither the Vendor nor the Auctioneers can accept any liability in respect of payments which may be outstanding in respect thereof or any responsibility in the matter whatsoever.

16. The Auctioneers reserve the right to sell in separate lots if the whole is unsold or sell in one lot where individual lots are offered. The Auctioneers reserve the right to sell prior to auction.

17. The Vendor reserves the right to alter or add to the said Particulars and Conditions of Sale at any time prior to the sale.

18. The Auctioneers reserve the right to hold the Memorandum of Contract signed by them, on behalf of the Vendors, until the Purchaser's cheque for the deposit has been cleared.

19. No objection or requisition shall be raised as to the permitted user of the property for the purpose of the Town and Country Planning Acts or any Act or Acts for the time being amended or replacing the same or as to any other matters arising under the said Acts or any Rules or Regulations made or arising thereunder and the Purchaser shall take the properties as they are under the said Acts, Rules and Regulations.

20. The only representation made or intended to be implied by or from the said Particulars in relation to tenancies is that the amounts of rents stated are the rents actually payable or being paid by the tenant to the Vendor and no representation is made that those rents are properly payable. No representation is made that any notices served were valid in proper form or properly served and the Vendor shall not be required to furnish copies of any notices served by him or his predecessors in Title, and shall not be liable to make compensation for any rents found to be improperly increased or not legally payable. The Purchaser shall be satisfied with such evidence or information of the terms of the tenancies as the Vendor can supply whether such have been reduced to writing or not.

◆ PROPERTY AUCTIONS ◆

The property is sold subject to and with the benefit of the tenancies referred to in the Particulars of Sale.

21. The Purchaser will satisfy himself before signing the contract as to the correctness of all rents, business or otherwise and as to whether the same are properly payable under or by virtue of current legislation and statutory instruments made thereunder and no objections, requisitions or enquiry shall be made by the Purchaser whether or not he has made such enquiries as to the correctness or otherwise of such rentals of any of them or that the same are not lawfully recoverable either in whole or in part and that the Purchaser shall not be entitled to refuse to complete or to demand compensation or damages in any way make any claim or counterclaim compensation on account of any of these matters.

22. Nothing shall be incorporated in any sale either collaterally or directly or indirectly whether by way of condition, warranty or representation as to whether, in the case of property sold subject to any tenancy or tenancies, there are subsisting any subtenancies or similar such occupations and whether or not any such shall be disclosed at or before the Auction the Purchaser shall be deemed to purchase with full knowledge of any such sub-tenancy or sub-tenancies or occupations that there may be whether or not he shall have enquired of the Auctioneers or have inspected and no objection shall be taken or requisition made on account thereof.

23. Nothing herein contained shall be deemed to constitute any warranty by the Vendor or the Auctioneers that the demised premises or any part thereof are authorised under the Planning Acts, Leases or otherwise for use for any specific purpose.

24. No Purchaser shall raise any objection or requisition or enquiry in respect of any rights, covenants, obligations, easements, privileges, licences, subsisting, acquiring or being acquired over under or in respect of the properties and the Vendors or the Auctioneers shall be under no liability to disclose the same whether or not the same are known to them.

25. The properties are sold subject to any charges, notices, orders, restrictions, agreements and matters affecting them under the Town and Country Planning Acts or any rules or regulations thereunder.

26. Each Purchaser will take the relevant property subject to and shall be responsible for the compliance with all notices and/or requirements relating to the same whether such notices and/or requirements shall have been made by the local authorities or any other person or body and whether as between landlord and tenant they are the liability of the landlord or of the tenant and whether the same be served or intimated before or after the date of the contract to purchase the property.

27. Notwithstanding anything in these conditions or in the Particulars contained or referred to no representation, warranty or condition, either collaterally, directly or indirectly, shall be made or implied howsoever arising either as to the state or condition of the properties or any part

◆ APPENDICES ◆

thereof or as to whether the same is subject to any resolutions, schemes, development orders, improvements plans, improvement notices or schemes, sanitary notices or intimation notices or proposals under the Housing Acts or any of them or as to whether any property is in an area where redevelopment is proposed or is subject to a road widening proposal or scheme or any other matter whatsoever. The Purchasers shall be deemed to purchase in all respects subject thereto whether or not they make any enquiry and neither the Vendors nor the Auctioneers shall be required or bound to inform the Purchasers of any such matters whether known to them or not and the Purchasers shall raise no enquiry, requisition or objection thereon or on any such matters as aforesaid and neither the Vendors nor the Auctioneers shall be in any way liable in respect of such matters or failure to disclose the same it being solely the duty of the Purchasers to satisfy themselves at their own risk in respect of the above matters.

28. No Purchaser shall make any requisition or objection in regard to any of the matters referred to in Clauses 9, 14, 15, 25 and 27 of these General Conditions and each Purchaser shall indemnify the respective Vendors in respect of any claims which have arisen or which may arise in regard thereto.

29. It shall be the Purchasers' responsibility to satisfy themselves before making a bid as to the accuracy of the Particulars contained in the Particulars of Sale.

30. The Purchaser hereby admits and confirms that the Purchaser
   (i) Has inspected the property
   (ii) Has obtained advice and information with regard thereto independently of the Vendor and the Auctioneers
   (iii) Has not been induced to enter into this agreement by or in reliance upon any statement either oral or in writing made by or on behalf of the Vendor.

31. Each Purchaser shall be deemed to be personally liable on making an accepted bid even though he shall purport to act as agent for a principal, and despite him purporting to sign a memorandum in a representative capacity, so that their liability under the contract shall be joint and several.

Appendix 3

Typical Catalogue Entries and Special Conditions for Commercial Property

Lot 1	Highly Reversionary Freehold Office Investment
	– Let to . . .
[Full Address]	– Valuable Reversion 20 years hence

Tenure

Freehold.

Location

North . . . is a prosperous residential and retail centre that is becoming increasingly important as an office location. The centre is situated some . . . miles north of Central London on the . . . providing access to the M1 motorway.

The property is situated south east of . . . in a mixed commercial and residential area.

Description

The property comprises an office building arranged on ground and two upper floors, having the benefit of rear access from. . . . The property is of traditional brick construction under a pitched slate roof and provides the following accommodation:

Ground Floor	640 sq.ft.
1st Floor	550 sq.ft.
2nd Floor	545 sq.ft.
Total:	1,735 sq.ft.

Tenancy

The entire property is let to . . . for a term of 99 years from 25th December, 1908 at a fixed rent of £18 per annum, exclusive of rates. The lease contains full repairing covenants.

Vendor's Solicitors	Low Current Rent Reserved per £18 annum	Joint Auctioneer
[Reference & full name, address and phone number]	(exclusive of rates) **Substantial Reversion 2007**	*[Full name, address and phone number]*

♦ APPENDICES ♦

Lot 2

**Long Leasehold Commercial Property
– Excellent West End Location
– Redevelopment Potential subject to Necessary Consents
– Full Vacant Possession upon Completion**

[Full Address]

Tenure

Leasehold – Held on a lease for a term of 125 years from 29th September 1984 at a current rent of £300 per annum, exclusive of rates, doubling every 33rd year of the term.

Location

... Street runs between ... Street and ... Street ... in the very heart of the West End. Oxford Circus, Tottenham Court Road and Goodge Street Underground Stations are all within walking distance of the property, and the comprehensive shopping facilities of Oxford Street are close by.

Description

The properties comprise a pair of period buildings of brick construction under pitched roofs, arranged on basement, ground and two upper floors. Both require extensive modernisation.

Possible future use could include office use subject to the necessary consents under the new Use Class 'B1 Business'. The following accommodation is provided:

No. 25:	Basement	300 sq.ft.
	Ground Floor	215 sq.ft.
	First Floor	285 sq.ft.
	Second Fl.	290 sq.ft.
	Total:	1,090 sq.ft. (net internal)

No. 27:	Basement	300 sq.ft.
	Ground Floor	275 sq.ft.
	First Floor	300 sq.ft.
	Second Fl.	290 sq.ft.
	Total:	1,165 sq.ft. (net internal)

Tenancy

Both properties are offered with FULL VACANT POSSESSION UPON COMPLETION.

Vendor's Solicitor	Joint Auctioneer
[Full name, address and phone number]	*[Full name, address and phone number]*

♦ PROPERTY AUCTIONS ♦

Lot 3

[Full Address]

Tenure

Freehold.

Location

... is a major retail, office and commercial centre having a population of 80,000 with an extensive catchment area. The town is located on the ... trunk road some ... miles north east of London. The High Street is the principal trading thoroughfare.

Description

This recently completed and attractive development comprises 2 shops, each having trading frontages to the High Street, and ancillary accommodation at first floor level. The building is of brick construction, part rendered to the front elevation, under pitched slate and tiled roofs.

First Class Freehold Shop Investment
– to be offered in one Lot

Accommodation and Tenancies

A Schedule of Acommodation and Tenancies is set out below.

No.	Lessee	Accommodation	Lease Terms	Current Rent £ p.a.	Review/ Reversion
1 (Unit 1)	... Ltd, with personal sureties (8 branches)	Gross Frontage 20' Net Frontage 18' Depth to steps 68'9" Built depth 94' 1st Fl. 600 sq.ft.	20 years from 25.12.83. Rent reviews every 5th year. F.R. & I. by way of service charge.	£17,750 p.a.	Rent Review 1992
2 (Unit 2)	... Ltd, with personal sureties t/a ... Restaurant (2 restaurants)	Gross Frontage 19'6" Net Frontage 18'6" Depth to steps 65'9" Built depth 92' 1st Fl. 525 sq.ft.	20 years from 25.12.83. Rent reviews every 5th year. F.R. & I. by way of service charge.	£18,250 p.a.	Rent Review 1992

Vendor's Solicitor *[Full name, address and phone number]*	Current Rents Reserved per £36,000 annum (exclusive of rates) **Rent Reviews from 1988**	Joint Auctioneer *[Full name, address and phone number]*

◆ APPENDICES ◆

Special Conditions of Sale

AS TO LOT I

[Full Address]

1. The Vendor's Solicitors are Messrs. . . .
2. The Property to be sold ('the Property') is the whole of the property which is registered at H.M. Land Registry with Title Absolute under Title Number. . . .
3. The Property is sold together with the benefit of but subject to the matters contained or referred to in the Property Register and subject to the matters contained or referred to in Entry Numbers 1 and 2 of the Charges Register of the above title.
4. In particular, as referred to in Entry Number 2 of the Charges Register, the Property is sold subject to and with the benefit of the following Lease:
A Lease dated 15th December 1908 (which now only relates to the land engaged yellow on the Filed Plan) for a term of 99 years from 25th December 1908. The rent payable under the Lease was apportioned under an Assignment dated 19th September 1952 whereby the land edged yellow on the Filed Plan was assigned to The Middlesex County Council for the remainder of the term. As regards the balance of the property comprised in the said Lease the Leasehold interest merged with the Freehold reversion and has been sold and is now registered under Title Number. . . . The Property is further sold together with the benefit of but subject to the matters contained in the aforesaid Assignment.
5. In the event of notice under National Condition 22 (as varied) of the National Conditions of Sale being served the Purchaser shall be and become liable to pay and indemnify the Vendor for its legal costs (on the solicitor and own client basis) of and incidental to the preparation and service of the said notice and all additional work consequent upon the Purchaser's default in completing on the contractual date such costs being in the minimum sum of Twenty-five pounds (£25.00) exclusive of V.A.T. and such sum shall be payable at completion with the balance of the purchase price, interest and any other sum due to the Vendor at completion.
6. The Purchaser shall in the Transfer enter into a Covenant by way of indemnity only to observe and perform the covenants on the part of the Lessor Contained in the Lease and to keep the Vendor fully indemnified against any breach or non-observance thereof.

Special Conditions of Sale

AS TO LOT 2

[Full Address]

1. The properties are registered under H.M. Land Registry with absolute leasehold title under titles numbered . . . and . . . . Title shall consist of office copy entries of the said title together with a copy of the transfer thereof in favour of the Vendor. The Vendor shall not be required to complete the registration of the transfer to the Vendor prior to completion but if such registration shall have been completed then title shall be deduced in accordance with the Land Registration Acts.
2. The property is sold subject to the terms of the Leases referred to in the property registers of the said titles and to the notes referred to therein and to

◆ PROPERTY AUCTIONS ◆

the matters set out or referred to in entry 1 of the charge register of each of the said titles. Copy entries and a copy of the transfer are available for inspection by prior appointment at the offices of the Vendors Solicitors Messrs . . . and whether inspected or not the purchaser shall be deemed to purchase with full knowledge thereof and shall raise no enquiries or requisitions thereon or objections thereto.

3. The property is sold with vacant possession on completion.
4. The Vendor sells as beneficial owner.
5. The prescribed rate of interest shall be 16% p.a.
6. Completion shall take place four weeks after the date of the auction (or the signing of a contract if earlier) at the offices of the Vendor's Solicitors as aforesaid or as they may direct.

Special Conditions of Sale

AS TO LOT 3

[Full Address]

1. The Vendor's Solicitors are Messrs . . . at whose offices copies of relevant documentation may be inspected and completion will take place.
2. The Vendor sells as Beneficial Owner.
3. The Title to the Property is registered at H.M. Land Registry with Title Absolute under Title Number . . . and the Property is sold subject to all matters referred to in the Property and Charges Registers of the said Title Number (save for any Mortgage) and the Purchaser shall be deemed to purchase with full notice and knowledge thereof and shall raise no enquiry, requisition or objection with regard thereto.
4. The Transfer of the property shall contain a covenant by the Purchaser with the Vendor that the Purchaser and its/his Successors in Title will at all times thereafter observe and perform the covenants conditions and obligations (whether expressed or implied) entered into by or imposed or binding on the Vendor as Landlord in the Leases to which the Property is subject and to indemnify and keep indemnified the Vendor and its Successors in Title against all actions, proceedings, costs, claims and demands whatsoever and howsoever arising in respect of any non-observance or non-performance thereof.
5. The National Conditions of Sale (20th Edition) shall be further varied as follows:
(a) There shall be excluded Condition 5(3)(iii).
(b) Proviso (i) to Condition 5(5) shall be altered to read 'for the purpose of conditions 6 and 7 if actual completion shall take place after 12.00 noon then the date of actual completion shall be taken to be the first working day thereafter.'
(c) In Condition 22(2) and (3) 'Ten working days' shall be substituted for 'sixteen working days'.
6. The deposit shall be paid to the Auctioneers as Agents for the Vendor.
7. In the event of there being any arrears of rent and/or any other payments due from any of the tenants as at the date of completion the Purchaser shall pay such arrears to the Vendor who will at the request and cost of the Purchaser assign to the Purchaser the right to claim such arrears.

Appendix 4

Particulars and Special Conditions of Sale for a Country Residential Property

SITUATION

The property lies off a private road in the quiet hamlet of . . . on the edge of . . . Forest surrounded by lovely wooded countryside. The Forest is principally made up of mature Beech woodland which totals in excess of 4,000 acres. . . . and . . . are about 5 and 8 miles distant respectively, whilst . . . provides fast access to London and the motorway network. The railway station with a direct service to London is about 2 miles distant.

HISTORICAL NOTE

The . . . Estate has been in the Marquess of . . .'s family since the eleventh century. Henry VIII used to hunt in the forest.

VIEWING

Strictly by appointment with the Auctioneers.

TENURE AND POSSESSION

The properties are FREEHOLD and VACANT POSSESSION will be given on completion with the exception of the small vegetable garden which will be vacated on 31 December 198 .

OUTGOINGS AND ASSESSMENTS

Property	Rateable Value	Rates payable as from 1.4.8-
Cottage No. 1	£58	£117.04
Cottage No. 2	£51	£102.92
Cottage No. 3	£63	£127.13

AUTHORITIES

District Council: [name, address and phone no.]
Planning & Home Improvement Grants: . . .
County Council: . . .
Water: . . .
Electricity: . . .

SALE PARTICULARS AND PLAN

1. The property is sold with all faults and defects whether of condition or otherwise and neither the Vendors . . . nor Messrs . . . are responsible

♦ PROPERTY AUCTIONS ♦

for any such faults or defects, or for any statements contained in the Particulars of the property by the said Agents.

2. The Purchaser shall be deemed to acknowledge that he has not entered into this contract in reliance on any of the said statements, that he has satisfied himself as to the correctness of each of the said statements by inspection or otherwise and no warranty or representation has been made by the Vendors or the said Agents in relation to or in connection with the property.

3. Any error, omission or mis-statement in any of the said statements, shall not entitle the Purchaser to rescind or to be discharged from his contract, nor entitle either party to compensation or damages nor in any circumstances give either party cause of action.

4. The plans and quantities are based on the relevant Ordnance Survey Sheets as revised by the Auctioneers. Where fields or enclosures have been divided, the areas have been estimated by the Auctioneers and the quantities are believed to be correct and shall be so accepted by the Purchaser.

RIGHTS, EASEMENTS AND OUTGOINGS

The property is sold subject to and with the benefit of all public and private rights of way, water, support, drainage, light and other rights and obligations, easements, quasi-easements and restrictive covenants, all existing and proposed wayleaves for electricity and telegraph poles and cables, masts, pylons, stays, drains and pipes whether mentioned in the Stipulations or Particulars or not. The Vendors shall not be required to define any such rights, easements, privileges or advantages.

FIXTURES AND FITTINGS

All fixtures usually denominated Landlord's fixtures belonging to the Vendors will be included in the sale. All fixtures and fittings denominated Tenant's fixtures and fittings belonging to the Vendors and remaining on the property on the date fixed for completion, will also be included in the sale price.

TOWN PLANNING

The property is situated in an Area of Outstanding Natural Beauty notwithstanding any description contained in the particulars, is sold subject to any structure plan, development plan, town planning scheme, resolution or notice which may be, or may come to be in force and also subject to any planning or bye-law consent, road widening or improvement schemes, land charges and any statutory provisions or bye-laws, without any obligation on the part of the Vendors to specify them.

◆ APPENDICES ◆

BOUNDARIES

The property being open to inspection, the Purchaser shall be deemed to have knowledge of the ownership of every tree, fence and boundary.

CONTRACT

The contract will be subject to the Particulars, Special Conditions of Sale, Stipulations and Revisionary Notices (if any) which may be issued before the sale and to any alterations announced at the sale. In the case of any inconsistency between these Stipulations and the Special Conditions of Sale, the latter shall prevail.

THE PROPERTY

The cottages, set in about 1.7 acres, date from the 19th Century and are built of brick and timber under a slate roof. They are in need of complete renovation and provide an unusual opportunity to create (subject to the necessary planning consents) a substantial house in this unique and sought after area. The accommodation briefly comprises:

COTTAGE NO. 1

Ground Floor
Kitchen about 9' × 9'7"
Living Room about 12' × 14'
Pantry about 9' 1" × 5' 3"

First Floor
Bedroom 1 about 5'5" × 8'9"
Bedroom 2 about 9'6" × 9'
Bedroom 3 about 12'8" × 14'7"

COTTAGE NO. 2

Ground Floor
Living room about 15' × 12'
Kitchen

First Floor
Bedroom 1 about 12' × 5'9"
Bedroom 2 about 12' × 9'1"
Bedroom 3 about 9'6" × 7'1"

COTTAGE NO. 3

Ground Floor
Living room about 13'7" × 13'4"
Drawing room about 10'3" × 10'1"
Kitchen about 10'10" × 8'10"

♦ PROPERTY AUCTIONS ♦

First Floor
Bedroom 1 about 10'5" × 10'4"
Bedroom 2 about 13'10" × 13'2"
Bedroom 3 about 13'9" × 6'2"

OUTSIDE

To the West of the cottages there is a substantial brick and slate building currently forming 5 stores. The gardens and grounds amount to about 1.7 acres which contain a number of ornamental shrubs and mature trees.

SERVICES

Mains electricity is connected to the property.
Mains water is connected to the property.
There is no foul drainage.
Telephone subject to British Telecom regulations.

SPECIAL CONDITIONS OF SALE

Definitions

1. The following expressions shall where the context so admits have the following meanings:

(a) 'The Property' means 1, 2 and 3 . . . comprising 1.7 acres or thereabouts forming part of enclosure number . . . on the Ordnance Survey Map 1923 to 1924 Edition and for the purpose of identification only shown edged red on the plan attached thereto, together with the rights specified in the First Schedule hereto.

(b) 'The Vendors' means the Trustees of the Estate.

(c) 'The National Conditions' means the National Conditions of Sale, Twentieth Edition.

(d) 'The Purchaser' means the purchaser of the Property within the meaning of the National Conditions and includes joint purchasers.

The National Conditions

2. (A) The property is sold subject to the following Conditions and to the National Conditions so far as the same are not varied by or inconsistent with the following conditions.

(B) A copy of the National Conditions will be open to inspection at the offices of the Vendor's solicitors, Messrs . . . and at the offices of the auctioneers, prior to the time of the sale and at the auction and the Purchaser, whether he inspects the same or requests production thereof or not, shall be deemed to have full knowledge of the contents of the National Conditions and shall be bound by them.

3. The National Conditions shall be modified in manner following (that is to say):

♦ APPENDICES ♦

(i) Conditions 3, 5(3)(iii), 7(1)(iii), 8(3), 8(4), 15(2), 15(3), 21(2) and 21(3) of the National Conditions shall not have effect.

(ii) Condition 5(3)(iv) of the National Conditions shall be deleted and the following inserted in its place: '(iv) Receipt in a particular bank or branch for the credit of a specified account by telegraphic or other direct transfer (as requested or agreed to by the Vendors' solicitors)'.

(iii) Condition 5(5)(i) of the National Conditions shall be deleted and the following inserted in its place: '5(5)(i) For the purposes of Conditions 6, 7 and 8 if the Purchaser is unable or unwilling to complete before 2.00 pm on the date of actual completion then the date of actual completion shall be taken to be the first working day thereafter'.

(iv) The period referred to in Condition 9(1) of the National Conditions shall be six working days and the second period in condition 9(3) thereof four working days.

(v) In condition 17(3) of the National Conditions the words 'whether' and 'or otherwise' shall be deleted.

(vi) In Condition 22 of the National Conditions the words 'sixteen working days' in the two places they occur shall be deleted and the words 'fourteen days' substituted therefor.

(vii) In condition 22(3) of the National Conditions the words 'unless the court otherwise directs' shall be deleted.

(viii) The words 'and any other loss occasioned to the Vendors directly or indirectly as a result of the Purchaser's refusal or failure to complete' shall be added at the end of Condition 22(3) of the National Conditions.

4. The prescribed rate for the purpose of the National Conditions shall be a rate per annum equivalent to 4% above Barclays Bank PLC base rate prevailing on the date herein fixed for completion.

Withdrawal

5. The Vendors may withdraw the Property without declaring the reserve price.

Deposit

6. The Purchaser shall at the close of the sale pay to the Auctioneers as agents for the Vendors a deposit of ten per cent of the purchase money.

Completion Date and Possession

7. The completion date shall be the Fifth day of August One thousand nine hundred and eighty. . . .

8. (1) The sale is with vacant possession on completion with the exception of the small vegetable garden, vacant possession of which will be given on 31 December 198 .

(2) The property in the crops produce and vegetables growing on or in the said land shall belong to and remain the property of the Vendors and the Vendors and their employees shall be entitled to remove the same from such vegetable garden at any time prior to 31 December 198 .

♦ PROPERTY AUCTIONS ♦

Tenure

9. The interest sold in the Property is the fee simple absolute in possession.

Title

10. The Vendors are selling as trustees for sale.
11. Title to the Property shall be deduced and shall commence with a Conveyance dated 29 September 1957 and made between . . . Estate Company Limited in Voluntary Liquidation and . . . being a Conveyance of (inter alia) the Property to the shareholders in the said . . . Estate Company Limited. And the Purchaser shall accept such Conveyance as a good root of title and shall make no requisition or objection in respect of the same.

General Encumbrances Affecting The Property

12. The Property is sold subject to:
    (1) The exceptions and reservations specified in the Second Schedule hereto which will be excepted and reserved in fee simple out of the Property in favour of the Vendors and their successors in title owners or owner of the . . . Estate.
    (2) All existing wayleaves or rights (if any) in favour of British Telecommunications the Electricity or other authorities whether by agreement or otherwise.
    (3) All rights of way, water, light, drainage and other easements (if any) affecting the same.
    (4) All overriding interests (if any) affecting the same.
    (5) All acts, matters, deeds or things registered or capable of registration as local land charges under the Land Charges Act 1925 as amended.
13. The Purchaser so as to bind so far as may be the Property into whosoever hands the same may come shall in the Conveyance of the Property to him (jointly and severally) covenant with the Vendors and their successors in title for the protection of such of the adjoining or neighbouring property of the Vendors comprised in the . . . Estate as is capable of being benefited thereby and each and every part thereof to observe and perform the restrictive and other covenants contained in the Third Schedule hereto.
14. In the Conveyance of the Property to the Purchaser the Vendors will covenant with the Purchaser that they the Vendors will not shoot game which is flying over the Property and will instruct all persons shooting game with their authority not to shoot game which is flying over the Property.
15. The following declarations shall be included in the Conveyance to the Purchaser:

'It is hereby agreed and declared that

◆ APPENDICES ◆

(a) The access and use of light and air to and for the property hereby conveyed and any dwellinghouse erection or thing for the time being erected and standing hereon upon and over the adjoining or neighbouring property of the Vendors is enjoyed under the express consent of the Vendors and the Vendors and their successors in title owner or owners of such adjoining or neighbouring property or any part or parts thereof may from time to time and at any time interfere with or destroy the access of light and air to the property hereby conveyed and any dwellinghouse erection building or thing by erecting a new building or new buildings or altering any existing building or buildings on such adjoining or neighbouring property of the Vendors without any formal reservation or consent.

(b) This Conveyance shall not include or operate as a grant or assurance of any rights of way liberties privileges easements rights or advantages whatsoever (other than the rights hereby expressly granted) over the adjoining or neighbouring property of the Vendors or any part thereof now or heretofore held or used occupied or enjoyed or reputed or known as part or parcel of the property hereby conveyed or any part thereof or appurtenant thereto.'

16. The Purchaser shall at his own expense execute a duplicate of the Conveyance of the Property to him attend to any necessary stamping thereof immediately after completion on behalf of the Vendors and hand the same over to the Vendors' Solicitors immediately thereafter.

General

17. Notwithstanding the completion of the sale of the Property any special or other condition to which effect is not given by the Conveyance to the Purchaser and which is capable of taking effect after completion shall remain in full force and effect.

18. The Purchaser hereby admits that he has inspected the Property and that this agreement sets out all the terms agreed between the parties and that he enters this agreement solely as a result of such inspection and not in reliance on any representation or warranty (written oral or implied) made by or on behalf of the Vendors other than the written replies to any Enquiries before Contract raised by the Purchaser's Solicitors in writing and answered by the Vendors' Solicitors in writing.

THE FIRST SCHEDULE

Rights and Easements to be Granted to the Purchaser

1. A right of way with or without vehicles at all times over and along the track hatched black on the plan attached hereto for the purpose of obtaining access to and egress from the Property from and to the public highway and for no other purposes.

2. The right to use all drains sewers watercourses pipes and telephone

◆ PROPERTY AUCTIONS ◆

electric and other wires or cables now serving the Property from the adjoining or neighbouring property of the Vendors comprised in the . . . Estate. And full and free right and liberty at all times hereafter upon reasonable prior notice in writing except in emergency to enter upon such adjoining or neighbouring property for the purpose of maintaining cleansing relaying renewing or repairing such drains sewers watercourses pipes and telephone electric and other wires or cables the person or persons exercising such rights doing as little damage as possible to such adjoining or neighbouring property and making good any damage done with expedition at his or their own expense.

3. All game woodcocks snipes quails landrail and other wild birds hens rabbits wildfowl and deer with the exclusive right for the Vendors and all persons authorised by them to enter upon all or any part of the Property for the purpose of picking up and recovering shot game.

THE SECOND SCHEDULE

Exceptions and Reservations

The right to use all drains sewers watercourses ditches pipes telephone or electric and other wires or cables as now run or proceed through the Property to or from the adjoining or neighbouring property of the Vendors comprised in the . . . Estate. And full and free right and liberty at all times hereafter upon reasonable prior notice in writing except in emergency to enter upon the Property for the purpose of maintaining cleansing relaying renewing or repairing any such drains sewers watercourses ditches pipes telephone or electric and other wires or cables the person or persons exercising such right doing as little damage as possible to the Property and making good any damage done with expedition at his or their own expense.

THE THIRD SCHEDULE

Restrictive and Other Covenants

1. At his own expense within three months of the date hereof in a good and workmanlike manner to the satisfaction of the Vendors to erect and forever thereafter to maintain stock proof fences constructed of posts with at least two rails along those boundaries of the property hereby conveyed between the points marked 'A' and 'B' and between the points marked 'C' and 'D' on the said plan.
2. Forever hereafter to maintain in good repair and condition to the satisfaction of the Vendors the fences on those boundaries of the property hereby conveyed marked with a 'T' inwards on the said plan.
3. At all times hereafter to maintain in good heart and condition the trees bushes shrubs and hedges on the roadside boundary of the property hereby conveyed and to replace any that die or are destroyed.

◆ APPENDICES ◆

4. Not to do or suffer to be done on the property hereby conveyed or any part thereof any act or thing which may be or grow to be a nuisance damage annoyance or inconvenience to the Vendors or their successors in title as aforesaid.

5. Not to obstruct or permit or suffer to be obstructed the road hatched black on the said plan.

6. Not to build erect or place or permit or allow to be built erected or placed on the property hereby conveyed or any part thereof any building (including any extension to an existing building) (whether temporary or permanent) hut shed caravan house on wheels or other structure (whether temporary or permanent) without the prior written consent of the Vendors or their successors in title as aforesaid and to allow the Vendors and their successors in title to demolish and remove the materials of any buildings huts sheds caravans houses on wheels or other structures erected or placed thereon without such consent as aforesaid and to indemnify the Vendors and their successors in title against all costs incurred in doing so.

7. Not to use the property hereby conveyed other than for residential purposes.

8. Not to carry out any development (as defined in the Town and Country Planning Act 1971) on any part of the property hereby conveyed without the prior written consent of the Vendors or their successors in title as aforesaid.

9. Subject to the provisions of the Ground Game Act 1880 as amended not to shoot destroy or disturb or to permit anyone to shoot destroy or disturb any game upon the property hereby conveyed nor to attempt to let or sell the shooting rights over the same.

Appendix 5

Memoranda of Sale and Purchaser's Slip

FOR THE AUCTION OF AN INDIVIDUAL RESIDENTIAL PROPERTY.

Memorandum

I/WE

of

do hereby acknowledge that I/we have this day purchased from . . . the property described in the foregoing Particulars of Sale for the sum of £ ....
and that I/we have paid the sum of £............. by way of deposit and in part payment of the said purchase money to Messrs . . . The Auctioneers, as agents for the Vendors, and I/we hereby agree to pay the remainder of the purchase money and complete the said purchase according to the foregoing Particulars of Sale and Special Conditions of Sale.

AS WITNESS my/our hand/s this   day of
                    One thousand nine hundred and eighty

Purchase money	£
Deposit	£
Balance payable	£

Signed (Purchaser/s) ....

As agents for the Vendors we acknowledge receipt of the said deposit and ratify the said sale.

....
(Auctioneers)

Solicitors acting for the Purchaser   ....
Ref: ....

◆ APPENDICES ◆

FOR AN AUCTION OF NUMEROUS COMMERCIAL PROPERTIES.

Memorandum

Auction 8 & 9 July 198

Lot
Address ....
....
....
....

I/WE
....

hereby acknowledge myself/ourselves to be the Purchaser(s) of the above Lot.
described in the foregoing Particulars at the sum of:
.... (£   )
and I/We have paid the sum of:
.... (£   )
to Messrs . . . as a deposit and in part payment of the purchase money. I/We agree to pay the remainder thereof and to complete the purchase in accordance with the annexed Particulars and Conditions of Sale in all respects.

DATE this   day of   198

Purchase money	£
Deposit	£
Balance	£

Signed by the Purchaser ....
As Agents for the Vendor ....
we ratify the Sale and acknowledge receipt of the above mentioned deposit in accordance with the Conditions of Sale.

Signed on behalf of the Vendor ....

Abstract of Title to be sent to: ....
....
....
....

DO NOT DETACH THIS PAGE FROM THE CATALOGUE

◆ PROPERTY AUCTIONS ◆

Messrs . . .   Auction   October 19

Purchaser's Slip

LOT.........

I/We acknowledge myself/ourselves to be the Purchaser of the above lot as set out in the aforegoing particulars and conditions of sale as amended by the addendum.

(1) Purchase Price £..

(2) Successful Bidder's full name, address and telephone no.:
....
....
Telephone Number..

(3) Purchaser's full name and address
    (if different from (2) above)
....
....
Telephone Number..

(4) Abstract Title to be sent to:
    (Purchaser's Solicitor's name and address)
....
....

Appendix 6

Catalogue Proof Check-List

SALE DATE 198

1ST/2ND/3RD PROOF

Proofs received from printer . . . [time] . . . [date]

Response received from clients/solicitors/joint auctioneers by . . . [time] . . . [date]

At first proof stage
– lotting order
– cover colour choice

COVER
– date

LOCATION MAP
– any enlarged area indicated as well as possible
– all towns marked
– town locations
– town spellings
– all lot numbers marked

TITLE PAGE
– number of lots
– description of all lots
– sale day/date
– sale time
– sale venue
– venue map needed?

ORDER OF SALE
– opening para includes wording 'unless sold previously'
– alignment of columns
– towns in upper case
– addresses in lower case
– totals correct with total lines
– page numbers correct
– 'Next Sales' announcement

NOTICE TO BIDDERS
– inserted and on r/h page
– page perforated
– sale date correct

PARTICULARS PAGES
Heading
– one comment each side –
full/brief enough

Addresses
– same as Special Conditions
– include joint auctioneers (not agents)

Maps
– shading of demise
– edge writing deleted
– lines clear
– north: direction
– writing of script
– streets in Letraset, well spaced
– for Goad: superfluous street numbers deleted
– for O. S.: superfluous hieroglyphics (bench mks. etc.) deleted

Photos
– alignment
– cropping
– size

Narrative
Order: location, description, accommodation, tenure, tenancies

Town data
– in separate paragraph to location of property in town

◆ PROPERTY AUCTIONS ◆

Description
- accommodation
- tenancies
- schedules
- tenure (subsidiary parts identified in heavier typeface)

Accommodation
- 'approximate dimensions and areas'
- dimensions given in separate columns to areas
- columns aligned

Accommodation/description/tenancies: brief, good, accurate wording

Box
- 'total gross income £. . . p.a. ex.'

Auctioneer's Note (*italics*)
- needed
- succinct/accurate

Photos/maps/box: relative sizes/position on page(s)

GENERAL CONDITIONS OF SALE
- numbering of clauses
- indenting consistent
- punctuation
- proof read

SPECIAL CONDITIONS OF SALE
- solicitor/address/ref/tel no./telex
- numbering of lots
- indenting consistent
- punctuation
- proof read
- consistency of singular/plural vendor wording *per lot*
- Vendor, Purchaser, Property: normally with cap V. etc.
- addresses per particulars [solicitor's word is binding]

MEMORANDUM
- room to write
- words 'not to be detached' included
- consistent space allowed for figures, etc.

General consistency throughout catalogue of
- boxes
- typefaces
- titles to photos, etc.
- non-particulars pages: headings, wording and colour
- joint auctioneers: names, addresses, tel nos., wording and colour

144

Appendix 7

Extracts from Statutes

AUCTIONEERS ACT 1845

. . .

Auctioneer, before he shall commence any Sale, shall suspend or affix a Ticket or Board containing his full Christian and Surname and Place of Residence

VII. And be it enacted, That every Auctioneer, before beginning any Auction, shall affix or suspend, or cause to be affixed or suspended, a Ticket or Board containing his true and full Christian and Surname and Residence painted, printed, or written in large Letters publicly visible and legible in some conspicuous Part of the Room or Place where the Auction is held, so that all Persons may easily read the same, and shall also keep such Ticket or Board so affixed or suspended during the whole Time of such Auction being held; and if any Auctioneer begins any Auction, or acts as Auctioneer at any Auction, in any Room or Place where his Name and Residence is not so painted or written on a Ticket or Board so affixed or suspended, and kept affixed or suspended as aforesaid, he shall forfeit for every such Offence the Sum of Twenty Pounds.

. . .

SALE OF LAND BY AUCTION ACT 1867

. . .

Interpretation of Terms

3. 'Auctioneer' shall mean any Person selling by Public Auction any Land, whether in Lots or otherwise:
   'Land' shall mean any Interest in any Messuages, Lands, Tenements, or Hereditaments of whatever Tenure:
   'Agent' shall mean the Solicitor, Steward, or Land Agent of the Seller:
   'Puffer' shall mean a Person appointed to bid on the Part of the Owner.

Where Sales are invalid in Law to be also invalid in Equity

4. 'And whereas there is at present a Conflict between Her Majesty's Courts of Law and Equity in respect of the Validity of Sales by Auction of Land where a Puffer has bid, although no Right of bidding on behalf of the Owner was reserved, the Courts of Law holding that all such Sales are absolutely illegal, and the Courts of Equity under some Circumstances giving effect to them, but even in Courts of Equity the Rule is unsettled: And whereas it is expedient that an End should be put to such conflicting and unsettled Opinions:' Be it therefore enacted, That from and after the

◆ PROPERTY AUCTIONS ◆

passing of this Act whenever a Sale by Auction of Land would be invalid at Law by reason of the Employment of a Puffer, the same shall be deemed invalid in Equity as well as at Law.

Rule respecting Sale without Reserve, &c

5. 'And whereas as Sales of Land by Auction are now conducted many of such Sales are illegal, and could not be enforced against an unwilling Purchaser, and it is expedient for the Safety of both Seller and Purchaser that such Sales should be so conducted as to be binding on both Parties:' Be it therefore enacted by the Authority aforesaid as follows: That the Particulars or Conditions of Sale by Auction of any Land shall state whether such Land will be sold without Reserve, or subject to a reserved Price, or whether a Right to bid is reserved; if it is stated that such Land will be sold without Reserve, or to that Effect, then it shall not be lawful for the Seller to employ any Person to bid at such Sale, or for the Auctioneer to take knowingly any Bidding from any such Person.

Rule respecting Sale subject to Right of Seller to bid as he may think proper

6. And where any Sale by Auction of Land is declared either in the Particulars or Conditions of such Sale to be subject to a Right for the Seller to bid, it shall be lawful for the Seller or any One Person on his Behalf to bid at such Auction in such Manner as he may think proper.

. . .

AUCTIONS (BIDDING AGREEMENTS) ACT 1927

Certain bidding agreements to be illegal

1. (1) If any dealer agrees to give, or gives, or offers any gift or consideration to any other person as an inducement or reward for abstaining, or for having abstained, from bidding at a sale by auction either generally or for any particular lot, or if any person agrees to accept, or accepts, or attempts to obtain from any dealer any such gift or consideration as aforesaid, he shall be guilty of an offence under this Act, and shall be liable on summary conviction to a fine not exceeding one hundred pounds, or to a term of imprisonment for any period not exceeding six months, or to both such fine and such imprisonment:

Provided that, where it is proved that a dealer has previously to an auction entered into an agreement in writing with one or more persons to purchase goods at the auction bonâ fide on a joint account and has before the goods were purchased at the auction deposited a copy of the agreement with the auctioneer, such an agreement shall not be treated as an agreement made in contravention of this section.

(2) For the purposes of this section the expression 'dealer' means a person who in the normal course of his business attends sales by auction for the purpose of purchasing goods with a view to reselling them.

♦ APPENDICES ♦

(3) In England and Wales a prosecution for an offence under this section shall not be instituted without the consent of the Attorney-General or the Solicitor-General.

Right of vendors to treat certain sales as fraudulent

2. Any sale at an auction, with respect to which any such agreement or transaction as aforesaid has been made or effected, and which has been the subject of a prosecution and conviction, may, as against a purchaser who has been a party to such agreement or transaction, be treated by the vendor as a sale induced by fraud:

Provided that a notice or intimation by the vendor to the auctioneer that he intends to exercise such power in relation to any sale at the auction shall not affect the obligation of the auctioneer to deliver the goods to the purchaser.

Copy of Act to be exhibited at sale.

3. The particulars which under section seven of the Auctioneers Act, 1845, are required to be affixed or suspended in some conspicuous part of the room or place where the auction is held shall include a copy of this Act, and that section shall have effect accordingly.

. . .

AUCTIONS (BIDDING AGREEMENTS) ACT 1969

Offences under Auctions (Bidding Agreements) Act 1927 to be indictable as well as triable summarily, and extension of time for bringing summary proceedings

1. (1) Offences under section 1 of the Auctions (Bidding Agreements) Act 1927 (which, as amended by the Criminal Justice Act 1967, renders a dealer who agrees to give, or gives, or offers a gift or consideration to another as an inducement or reward for abstaining, or for having abstained, from bidding at a sale by auction punishable on summary conviction with a fine not exceeding £400 or imprisonment for a term not exceeding six months, or both, and renders similarly punishable a person who agrees to accept, or accepts, or attempts to obtain from a dealer any such gift or consideration as aforesaid) shall be triable on indictment as well as summarily; and the penalty that may be imposed on a person on conviction on indictment of an offence under that section shall be imprisonment for a term not exceeding two years or a fine or both.

. . .

Persons convicted not to attend or participate in auctions

2. (1) On any such summary conviction or conviction on indictment as is mentioned in section 1 above, the court may order that the person so

convicted or that person and any representative of him shall not (without leave of the court) for a period from the date of such conviction—

(a) in the case of a summary conviction, of not more than one year, or
(b) in the case of a conviction on indictment, of not more than three years,

enter upon any premises where goods intended for sale by auction are on display or to attend or participate in any way in any sale by auction.

(2) In the event of a contravention of an order under this section, the person who contravenes it (and, if he is the representative of another, that other also) shall be guilty of an offence and liable—

(a) on summary conviction, to a fine not exceeding £400;
(b) on conviction on indictment, to imprisonment for a term not exceeding two years or to a fine or to both.

(3) In any proceedings against a person in respect of a contravention of an order under this section consisting in the entry upon premises where goods intended for sale by auction were on display, it shall be a defence for him to prove that he did not know, and had no reason to suspect, that goods so intended were on display on the premises, and in any proceedings against a person in respect of a contravention of such an order consisting in his having done something as the representative of another, it shall be a defence for him to prove that he did not know, and had no reason to suspect, that that other was the subject of such an order.

(4) A person shall not be guilty of an offence under this section by reason only of his selling property by auction or causing it to be so sold.

Rights of seller of goods by auction where agreement subsists that some person shall abstain from bidding for the goods

3. (1) Where goods are purchased at an auction by a person who has entered into an agreement with another or others that the other or the others (or some of them) shall abstain from bidding for the goods (not being an agreement to purchase the goods bona fide on a joint account) and he or the other party, or one of the other parties, to the agreement is a dealer, the seller may avoid the contract under which the goods are purchased.

(2) Where a contract is avoided by virtue of the foregoing subsection, then, if the purchaser has obtained possession of the goods and restitution thereof is not made, the persons who were parties to the agreement that one or some of them should abstain from bidding for the goods the subject of the contract shall be jointly and severally liable to make good to the seller the loss (if any) he sustained by reason of the operation of the agreement.

♦ APPENDICES ♦

. . .

(4) Section 2 of the Auctions (Bidding Agreements) Act 1927 (right of vendors to treat certain sales as fraudulent) shall not apply to a sale the contract for which is made after the commencement of this Act.

(5) In this section, 'dealer' has the meaning assigned to it by section 1(2) of the Auctions (Bidding Agreements) Act 1927.

Copy of Act to be exhibited at sale

4. Section 3 of the Auctions (Bidding Agreements) Act 1927 (copy of Act to be exhibited at sale) shall have effect as if the reference to that Act included a reference to this Act.

. . .

MISREPRESENTATION ACT 1967

Removal of certain bars to rescission for innocent misrepresentation

1. Where a person has entered into a contract after a misrepresentation has been made to him, and—

   (a) the misrepresentation has become a term of the contract; or
   (b) the contract has been performed;

or both, then, if otherwise he would be entitled to rescind the contract without alleging fraud, he shall be so entitled, subject to the provisions of this Act, notwithstanding the matters mentioned in paragraphs (a) and (b) of this section.

Damages for misrepresentation

2.—(1) Where a person has entered into a contract after a misrepresentation has been made to him by another party thereto and as a result thereof he has suffered loss, then, if the person making the misrepresentation would be liable to damages in respect thereof had the misrepresentation been made fraudulently, that person shall be so liable notwithstanding that the misrepresentation was not made fraudulently, unless he proves that he had reasonable ground to believe and did believe up to the time the contract was made that the facts represented were true.

(2) Where a person has entered into a contract after a misrepresentation has been made to him otherwise than fraudulently, and he would be entitled, by reason of the misrepresentation, to rescind the contract, then, if it is claimed, in any proceedings arising out of the contract, that the contract ought to be or has been rescinded, the court or arbitrator may declare the contract subsisting and award damages in lieu of rescission, if of opinion that it would be equitable to do so, having regard to the nature of the misrepresentation and the loss that would be caused by it if the

contract were upheld, as well as to the loss that rescission would cause to the other party.

(3) Damages may be awarded against a person under subsection (2) of this section whether or not he is liable to damages under subsection (1) thereof, but where he is so liable any award under the said subsection (2) shall be taken into account in assessing his liability under the said subsection (1).

Avoidance of provision excluding liability for misrepresentation

3. If a contract contains a term which would exclude or restrict—

(a) any liability to which a party to a contract may be subject by reason of any misrepresentation made by him before the contract was made; or
(b) any remedy available to another party to the contract by reason of such a misrepresentation,

that term shall be of no effect except in so far as it satisfies the requirement of reasonableness as stated in section 11(1) of the Unfair Contract Terms Act 1977; and it is for those claiming that the term satisfies that requirement to show that it does.

. . .

UNFAIR CONTRACT TERMS ACT 1977

. . .

Effect of breach

9.—(1) Where for reliance upon it a contract term has to satisfy the requirement of reasonableness, it may be found to do so and be given effect accordingly notwithstanding that the contract has been terminated either by breach or by a party electing to treat it as repudiated.

(2) Where on a breach the contract is nevertheless affirmed by a party entitled to treat it as repudiated, this does not of itself exclude the requirement of reasonableness in relation to any contract term.

Evasion by means of secondary contract

10. A person is not bound by any contract term prejudicing or taking away rights of his which arise under, or in connection with the performance of, another contract, so far as those rights extend to the enforcement of another's liability which this Part of this Act prevents that other from excluding or restricting.

The 'reasonableness' test

11.—(1) In relation to a contract term, the requirement of reasonableness for the purposes of this Part of this Act, section 3 of the Misrepresentation

♦ APPENDICES ♦

Act 1967 and section 3 of the Misrepresentation Act (Northern Ireland) 1967 is that the term shall have been a fair and reasonable one to be included having regard to the circumstances which were, or ought reasonably to have been, known to or in the contemplation of the parties when the contract was made.

(2) In determining for the purposes of section 6 or 7 above whether a contract term satisfies the requirement of reasonableness, regard shall be had in particular to the matters specified in Schedule 2 to this Act; but this subsection does not prevent the court or arbitrator from holding, in accordance with any rule of law, that a term which purports to exclude or restrict any relevant liability is not a term of the contract.

(3) In relation to a notice (not being a notice having contractual effect), the requirement of reasonableness under this Act is that it should be fair and reasonable to allow reliance on it, having regard to all the circumstances obtaining when the liability arose or (but for the notice) would have arisen.

(4) Where by reference to a contract term or notice a person seeks to restrict liability to a specified sum of money, and the question arises (under this or any other Act) whether the term or notice satisfies the requirement of reasonableness, regard shall be had in particular (but without prejudice to subsection (2) above in the case of contract terms) to—

(a) the resources which he could expect to be available to him for the purpose of meeting the liability should it arise; and
(b) how far it was open to him to cover himself by insurance.

(5) It is for those claiming that a contract term or notice satisfies the requirement of reasonableness to show that it does.

'Dealing as consumer'

12.—(1) A party to a contract 'deals as consumer' in relation to another party if—

(a) he neither makes the contract in the course of a business nor holds himself out as doing so; and
(b) the other party does make the contract in the course of a business; and
(c) in the case of a contract governed by the law of sale of goods or hire-purchase, or by section 7 of this Act, the goods passing under or in pursuance of the contract are of a type ordinarily supplied for private use or consumption.

(2) But on a sale by auction or by competitive tender the buyer is not in any circumstances to be regarded as dealing as consumer.

(3) Subject to this, it is for those claiming that a party does not deal as consumer to show that he does not.

Varieties of exemption clause

13.—(1) To the extent that this Part of this Act prevents the exclusion or restriction of any liability it also prevents—

(*a*) making the liability or its enforcement subject to restrictive or onerous conditions;
(*b*) excluding or restricting any right or remedy in respect of the liability, or subjecting a person to any prejudice in consequence of his pursuing any such right or remedy;
(*c*) excluding or restricting rules of evidence or procedure; and (to that extent) sections 2 and 5 to 7 also prevent excluding or restricting liability by reference to terms and notices which exclude or restrict the relevant obligation or duty.

(2) But an agreement in writing to submit present or future differences to arbitration is not to be treated under this Part of this Act as excluding or restricting any liability.

SCHEDULE 2
'Guidelines' for Application of Reasonableness Test

The matters to which regard is to be had in particular for the purposes of sections 6(3), 7(3) and (4), 20 and 21 are any of the following which appear to be relevant—

(*a*) the strength of the bargaining positions of the parties relative to each other, taking into account (among other things) alternative means by which the customer's requirements could have been met;
(*b*) whether the customer received an inducement to agree to the term, or in accepting it had an opportunity of entering into a similar contract with other persons, but without having to accept a similar term;
(*c*) whether the customer knew or ought reasonably to have known of the existence and extent of the term (having regard, among other things, to any custom of the trade and any previous course of dealing between the parties);
(*d*) where the term excludes or restricts any relevant liability if some condition is not complied with, whether it was reasonable at the time of the contract to expect that compliance with that condition would be practicable;
(*e*) whether the goods were manufactured, processed or adapted to the special order of the customer.

. . .

♦ APPENDICES ♦
ESTATE AGENTS ACT 1979

. . .

Clients' money held on trust or as agent

13.—(1) It is hereby declared that clients' money received by any person in the course of estate agency work in England, Wales or Northern Ireland—

(a) is held by him on trust for the person who is entitled to call for it to be paid over to him or to be paid on his direction or to have it otherwise credited to him, or

(b) if it is received by him as stakeholder, is held by him on trust for the person who may become so entitled on the occurrence of the event against which the money is held.

. . .

Keeping of client accounts

14.—(1) Subject to such provision as may be made by accounts regulations, every person who receives clients' money in the course of estate agency work shall, without delay, pay the money into a client account maintained by him or by a person in whose employment he is.

(2) In this Act a 'client account' means a current or deposit account which—

(a) is with an institution authorised for the purposes of this section, and
(b) is in the name of a person who is or has been engaged in estate agency work; and
(c) contains in its title the word 'client'.

. . .

(8) A person who—

(a) contravenes any provision of this Act or of accounts regulations as to the manner in which clients' money is to be dealt with or accounts and records relating to such money are to be kept, or
(b) fails to produce an auditor's report when required to do so by accounts regulations,

shall be liable on summary conviction to a fine not exceeding £500.

. . .

Interest on clients' money

. . .

15.—(3) Except as provided by accounts regulations and subject to subsection (4) below, a person who maintains a client account in which he keeps clients' money generally shall not be liable to account to any person for interest received by him on money in that account.

♦ PROPERTY AUCTIONS ♦

(4) Nothing in this section or in accounts regulations shall affect any arrangement in writing, whenever made, between a person engaged in estate agency work and any other person as to the application of, or of any interest on, money in which that other person has or may have an interest.

. . .

Information to clients of prospective liabilities

18.—(1) Subject to subsection (2) below, before any person (in this section referred to as 'the client') enters into a contract with another (in this section referred to as 'the agent') under which the agent will engage in estate agency work on behalf of the client, the agent shall give the client—

. . .

(2) . . .

(a) particulars of the circumstances in which the client will become liable to pay remuneration to the agent for carrying out estate agency work;
(b) particulars of the amount of the agent's remuneration for carrying out estate agency work or, if that amount is not ascertainable at the time the information is given, particulars of the manner in which the remuneration will be calculated;
(c) particulars of any payments which do not form part of the agent's remuneration for carrying out estate agency work or a contract or precontract deposit but which, under the contract referred to in subsection (1) above, will or may in certain circumstances be payable by the client to the agent or any other person and particulars of the circumstances in which any such payments will become payable; and
(d) particulars of the amount of any payment falling within paragraph (c) above or, if that amount is not ascertainable at the time the information is given, an estimate of that amount together with particulars of the manner in which it will be calculated.

(3) If, at any time after the client and the agent have entered into such a contract as is referred to in subsection (1) above, the parties are agreed that the terms of the contract should be varied so far as they relate to the carrying out of estate agency work or any payment falling within subsection (2)(c) above, the agent shall give the client details of any changes which, at the time the statement is given, fall to be made in the information which was given to the client under subsection (1) above before the contract was entered into.

. . .

♦ APPENDICES ♦

Regulation of pre-contract deposits outside Scotland

19.—(1) No person may, in the course of estate agency work in England, Wales or Northern Ireland, seek from any other person (in this section referred to as a 'prospective purchaser') who wishes to acquire an interest in land in the United Kingdom, a payment which, if made, would constitute a pre-contract deposit in excess of the prescribed limit.

(2) If, in the course of estate agency work, any person receives from a prospective purchaser a pre-contract deposit which exceeds the prescribed limit, so much of that deposit as exceeds the prescribed limit shall forthwith be either repaid to the prospective purchaser or paid to such other person as the prospective purchaser may direct.

(3) In relation to a prospective purchaser, references in subsections (1) and (2) above to a pre-contract deposit shall be treated as references to the aggregate of all the payments which constitute pre-contract deposits in relation to his proposed acquisition of a particular interest in land in the United Kingdom.

(4) In this section 'the prescribed limit' means such limit as the Secretary of State may by regulations prescribe; and such a limit may be so prescribed either as a specific amount or as a percentage or fraction of a price or other amount determined in any particular case in accordance with the regulations.

Transactions in which an estate agent has a personal interest

21.—(1) A person who is engaged in estate agency work (in this section referred to as an 'estate agent') and has a personal interest in any land shall not enter into negotiations with any person with respect to the acquisition or disposal by that person of any interest in that land until the estate agent has disclosed to that person the nature and extent of his personal interest in it.

. . .

Standards of competence

22.—(1) The Secretary of State may by regulations made by statutory instrument make provision for ensuring that persons engaged in estate agency work satisfy minimum standards of competence.

. . .

THE PRECEDING STATUTORY MATERIAL IS CROWN COPYRIGHT.

Index

access routes, 56, 87
accounts, computerised, 9
advertising, 5–6, 23–5, 86, 105
agreement between vendor and auctioneer, 18–20
agricultural property, 78
  accommodation land, 80
  advantages of sale by auction, 83
  agents, 83–4
  auctioneers' qualifications, 91
  auction procedure:
    planning, 85
    preliminary instruction and sale report, 84–5
    preparation of the particulars 86–91
    timing and promotion, 85–6
  building land, 80
  buyers, 82
  estates, 79
  farms, 79–80, 87–9
  moorland, 80
  sporting rights, 79, 80–81
  vendors, 81–2
agricultural tenancy, 56
ancient monuments, 89
anonymity, 26–7, 103
auction departments:
  administration, 6–8
  computers, 9–10
  finance, 8–9
  inspection of property, 4
  instruction by clients, 3–4
  legal documents, 4–5
  marketing, 5–6
  multi-department practices, 12–14
  staffing, 10–12
  valuation, 5
auctioneers:
  agricultural properties, 91

assistants, 25
code of conduct *see* conduct of auctioneers
fees, 8, 100
knowledge of legislation, 25
personal promotion, 25
personal qualities, xiii–xiv, 12
qualifications, xiii
Auctioneers Act 1845, 93, 145
auctions:
  administration, 6–8
  advertising and public relations, 23–5
  agreement between vendor and auctioneer, 18–20
  agricultural property *see* agricultural property
  bidding *see* bidding
  contact with vendor's solicitors, 20–1
  cost of mounting, xiv, 106
  date, 15
  guide prices, 23
  industrial property *see* industrial property
  lead times, 16
  market trends, 1–3
  preparation of particulars, 21–3
  private, 38–9
  property inspection *see* inspection of property
  reserve price *see* reserve price
  residential investment, 45–8
  residential land, 57–8
  staff at the sale, 25–6
  statutes affecting conduct *see* legislation
  venue, 15
  weekly record of, x

◆ INDEX ◆

Auctions (Bidding Agreements) Acts, 93, 146–9

beneficiaries, 28, 33, 36
bidding:
  by telephone, 29
  controlling the level of, 27–8
  identifying the successful bidder, 27
  methods, 26–7
  'off the wall', 97–9
  on behalf of purchasers, 29
  residential investments, 45–6
  withdrawn bids, 29
booking auction rooms *see* room hire
boundaries, 55, 87
British Rail Property Board, 42, 43, 104, 106
brochures *see* catalogue
building land, 80, 104 *see also* residential land
building societies, 106–7
buyer's premium, 100

Capital Allowance Act 1968, 89
catalogue:
  as part of contract of sale, 21
  commercial properties, 126–8
  computerised drafting, 9
  distribution, xiv, 33, 43, 57, 61
  incorrect information, 21
  postage costs, 106
  preparation, 16–17
  profits for printing companies, 105
  proof check-list, 143–4
  residential investments, 42–3
  residential land, 50–2, 57–8
  see also particulars of sale
Chartered Auctioneers and Estate Agents' Institute, vii, ix
chartered surveyors, 101
check-lists
  catalogue preparation, 17, 143–4
  essential activities for a single property, 7
  updating by computer, 9
closing orders, 43
commercial property, 2, 13, 59–60, 68
  property companies, 64–7

reserve price, 62–4
retail groups, 67–8
Special Conditions of Sale, 129–30
suitability for auction, 60–2
typical catalogue entries, 126–8
vendors, 64
computers, 9–10
Conditions of Sale, 20, 103
  General, 120–5
  National, 20, 28, 108–19
  Special, 129–30, 134–9
  see also disclaimers
conduct of auctioneers, 95–6
  bidding 'off the wall', 97–9
  effect on market trends, 102–3
  fees, buyer's premium, 100
  lots sold or withdrawn prior to auction, 99
  price guides, 99
  purchase and sale of lots by interested parties, 100
  unsold lots, 96–7
confidentiality, 103
contracts between vendor and auctioneer, 18–20
country property, 37, 131–9 *and see* agricultural property
criminal liability, 97–9
crops, valuation of, 88
cultivated land, valuation of, 88

dangerous premises, 23
databases, 9
date of the auction, 15
deposits, 8, 20, 26
derelict premises, 23
development sites *see* residential land
disclaimers, 21, 43–4, 94
disclosed reserves, 28, 38
documents *see* legal documents
drainage, 87
Dutch auctions, 30

easements, 56, 87
electricity supply, 56, 87–8
Estate Agents Act 1979, 18, 95, 100, 153–5
exclusion clauses *see* disclaimers
exemption clauses *see* disclaimers

157

◆ INDEX ◆

expenses charged to vendors, 8, 18–20

farmers, 82
farmland, 79–80, 87–9
fees, 8, 18–20, 100
fiduciary clients, 32–3, 38 see also trustees
finance of auction departments, 8–9
fishing rights, 79, 80
Flight v Booth (1834) 1 Bing NC 370, 21
flooding, 55
forested land, 79, 87–8, 89
'For Sale' boards, 24, 86
fund managers, 70

gazumping, 31, 38
General Conditions of Sale, 120–5
gravel extraction, 55–6
grazing agreements, 56
guide prices, 23
gypsies, 56

Heakley v Newton (1881), 98
Health Authorities, 42, 43
house building land see residential land
Housing Acts, 43, 44

impartiality, 99–100
improvement notices, 46
incorrect information, 21, 44, 94
industrial property:
 categories, 71–3
 investment potential, 69–70
 nursery units, 77
 potential purchasers, 76
 preparation for auction, 74–6
 residential holdings, 42, 43
 retail warehouses, 77
 terraces of units, 76–7
 vacant buildings, 73–4
inspection of property, 4
 agricultural property, 87–8
 preparation of particulars, 21–3
 residential land, 55–6
investment properties, 2, 22
 see also residential properties

joint sales, 54–5

journal advertisements, 23–4, 105

King Brothers (Finance) Ltd v North Western British Road Services Ltd [1986] 2 EGLR 253, 21

Landlord and Tenant Acts, 25, 44–5
landowners, 82
Law of Property Act 1925, 95–6
Law Society's General Conditions of Sale, 20
lead times, 16, 86–91
leases, 22
legal documents, 4–5, 20–1, 56
legislation:
 Auctioneers Act 1845, 93, 145
 Auctions (Bidding Agreements) Acts, 93, 146–9
 Capital Allowance Act 1968, 89
 Estate Agents Act 1979, 18, 95, 100, 153–5
 Housing Acts, 43, 44
 Landlord and Tenant Acts, 25, 44–5
 Law of Property Act 1925, 95–6
 Misrepresentation Act 1967, 94, 149–50
 Occupiers Liability Act 1957, 23
 Public Health Acts, 43
 Rent Acts, 25, 105
 Sale of Land by Auction Acts, 92, 98, 145–6
 Theft Act 1968, 94
 Town and Country Planning Act 1971, 53
 Town and Country Planning General Development Order 1977, 89
 Unfair Contract Terms Act 1977, 94–5, 150–2
 Use Classes Order 1987, 75–6, 77
liability of auctioneers, 21, 43–4, 94, 97–9
listed buildings, 43–4, 89
local authorities' sale of land, 82
local press, 24, 86
location of auctions, 15–16, 43
London Auction Mart, ix–xi, xiii, 15, 100, 102–3, 106

mailing lists, 9, 24

◆ INDEX ◆

malpractice *see* conduct of auctioneers
marketing, 5–6, 23–5, 56–7, 85–6
market trends:
    affected by conduct of individual auctioneers, 102–3
    instruction by clients, 3–4
    opportunities for sale by auction, 1–3
    property market, 103–6
memoranda of sale, 26, 140–1
Metropolitan Police, 42, 106
mineral extraction, 55–6
misleading information, 21, 44, 94
Misrepresentation Act 1967, 94, 149–50
moorland, 80

National Coal Board, 43
National Conditions of Sale, 20, 28, 108–19
negligence, 21
newspaper advertisements, 24, 86, 105
notices, statutory, 43, 44, 46–7
nursery units, 77

occupation of development sites, 56
Occupiers Liability Act 1957, 23
Office of Fair Trading, 98, 99
Ordnance Survey, 88, 89
outstanding notices, 43

paddocks, 80
Parfitt v Jepson, 98
particulars of sale, 21–3, 33, 131–4
    agricultural properties, 86–91
    misleading or incorrect information, 21
    see also catalogue
pension funds, 103–4
photography, 50–1, 85
planning permissions, 52–4, 75–6, 85
pre-arranged bidding, 26–7, 103
pre-auction sales, 39–40, 99
press advertising, 23–4, 86
price:
    guides, 23, 99
    reserve *see* reserve price
printers:
    catalogue preparation, 16–17, 105
    computerisation, 9–10

private auctions, 38–9
private property companies, 64–5
private treaty sale, advantages and disadvantages of, 31–5
property *see* agricultural property, commercial property, industrial property, inspection of property, investment properties, residential properties
property companies, 64–7, 76
property market, 103–6
public authorities' sale of land and property, 42, 43, 82
public companies, chartered surveyors' incorporation as, 101
Public Health Acts, 43
public property companies, 65–7
public relations, 23–5
purchaser's slip, 142

radio advertisements, 24
Rent Acts, 25, 105
rent control, 41
reserve price, 23
    commercial property, 62–4
    disclosed, 28, 38
    fixing, 62–4
    last minute change, 28
    residential investment, 45
    sealed, 28–9
residential land, 49
    auction procedure, 57–8
    brochure presentation, 50–2
    inspection, 55–6
    joint sales, 54–5
    marketing, 56–7
    planning permissions, 52–4
    preliminary information, 50
    prices, 104
residential properties:
    individual, 31–2
    advantages and disadvantages of sale by auction, 32–5
    inspection, 22
    particulars for, 33, 131–4
    pre-auction sales, 39–40
    private auctions, 38–9
    Special Conditions for, 34, 134–9
    vendors, 35–6

♦ INDEX ♦

when to sell by auction, 36–8
investment:
   auction catalogue and location, 42–3
   auction results, 48
   bidding, 45–6
   reserve price, 45
   searches and pre-auction preparation, 43–5
   supply and demand, 41–2
retail groups, 67–8
retail warehouses, 77
rights of way, 56, 87
Rignall Developments v Halil [1987] 1 EGLR 193, 44
room hire, 6, 15–16
Royal Institution of Chartered Surveyors, x, 24, 101
runners, 26, 27
rural properties *see* agricultural property
sale:
   by tender, 31–2
   conditions of *see* Conditions of Sale
   particulars *see* particulars of sale
   relative advantages of auction and private treaty, 31–5
Sale of Land by Auction Acts, 92, 98, 145–6
Schedule of Dilapidations, 22
scientific interest, sites of, 89
Scotland, 3, 106
sealed reserves, 28–9
searches, 4, 20, 43–5, 50
security of tenure, 41, 56
shop investments, 60, 105
   property auctioned by retail groups, 67–8
sites of scientific interest, 89
soil surveys, 55
sole auctioneers, 13
solicitors, vendor's, 20–1
South Western General Property Co Ltd v Marton (1982) 263 EG 1090, 94
Special Conditions of Sale, 129–30, 134–9
sporting rights, 79, 80–1

spotters, 25
squatters, 56
statutes *see* legislation
statutory notices, 43, 44, 46–7
Stock Exchange, deregulation of, 101
surveyors, incorporation of, 101

telephone bidding, 29
television advertisements, 24
tenanted houses, demand for, 105 *see also* residential property, security of tenure
tender documents, 31–2
Theft Act 1968, 94
Topfell Ltd v Galley Properties Ltd (1978) 249 EG 341, 44
Town and Country Planning Act 1971, 53
Town and Country Planning General Development Order 1977, 89
transatlantic auctions, 3
tree preservation orders, 43–4, 55, 89
trustees, 36, 38, 81–2

Unfair Contract Terms Act 1977, 94–5, 150–2
unimproved properties, 37
unsold lots, 96–7
unusual properties, 37
Use Classes Order 1987, 75–6, 77

vacant possession, 31, 106
   reversionary value, 41
vacant properties, 2
   demand, 105
   industrial buildings, 73–4
valuation, 5, 88
venue of auctions, 15–16, 43
video-linked auctions, 3

warehouses, 77
warranty, 46, 94
water supply, 56, 87–8
withdrawn lots, 99
woodland, 79, 87–8, 89